MAKER

DESIGN A GAME!

COMICS

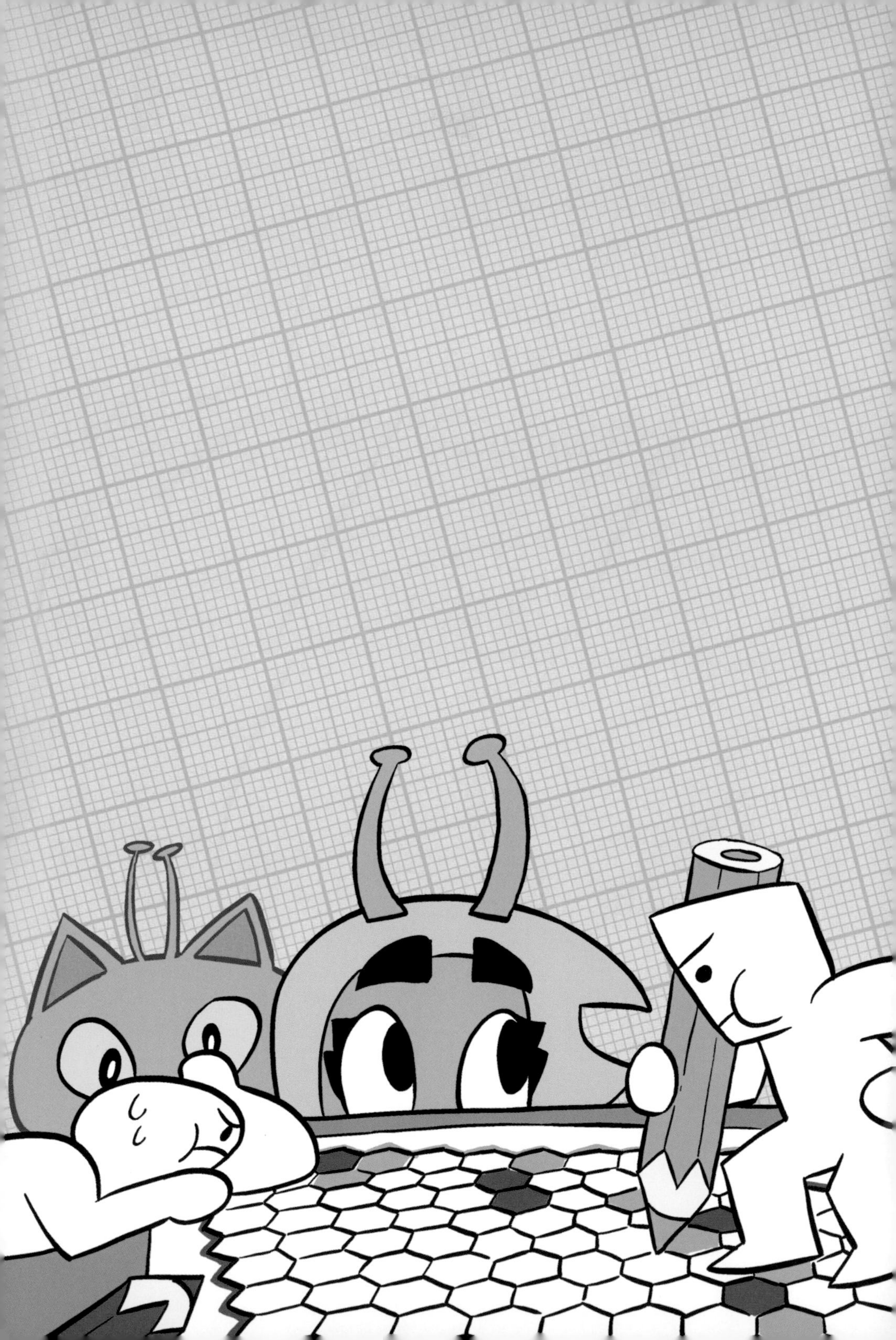

MAKER COMICS

DESIGN A GAME!

Written by Bree Wolf and Jesse Fuchs

Art by Bree Wolf

LV1
LV1
HP: 75
SPD:10
STR:12
DEF: 8

:01
First Second
New York

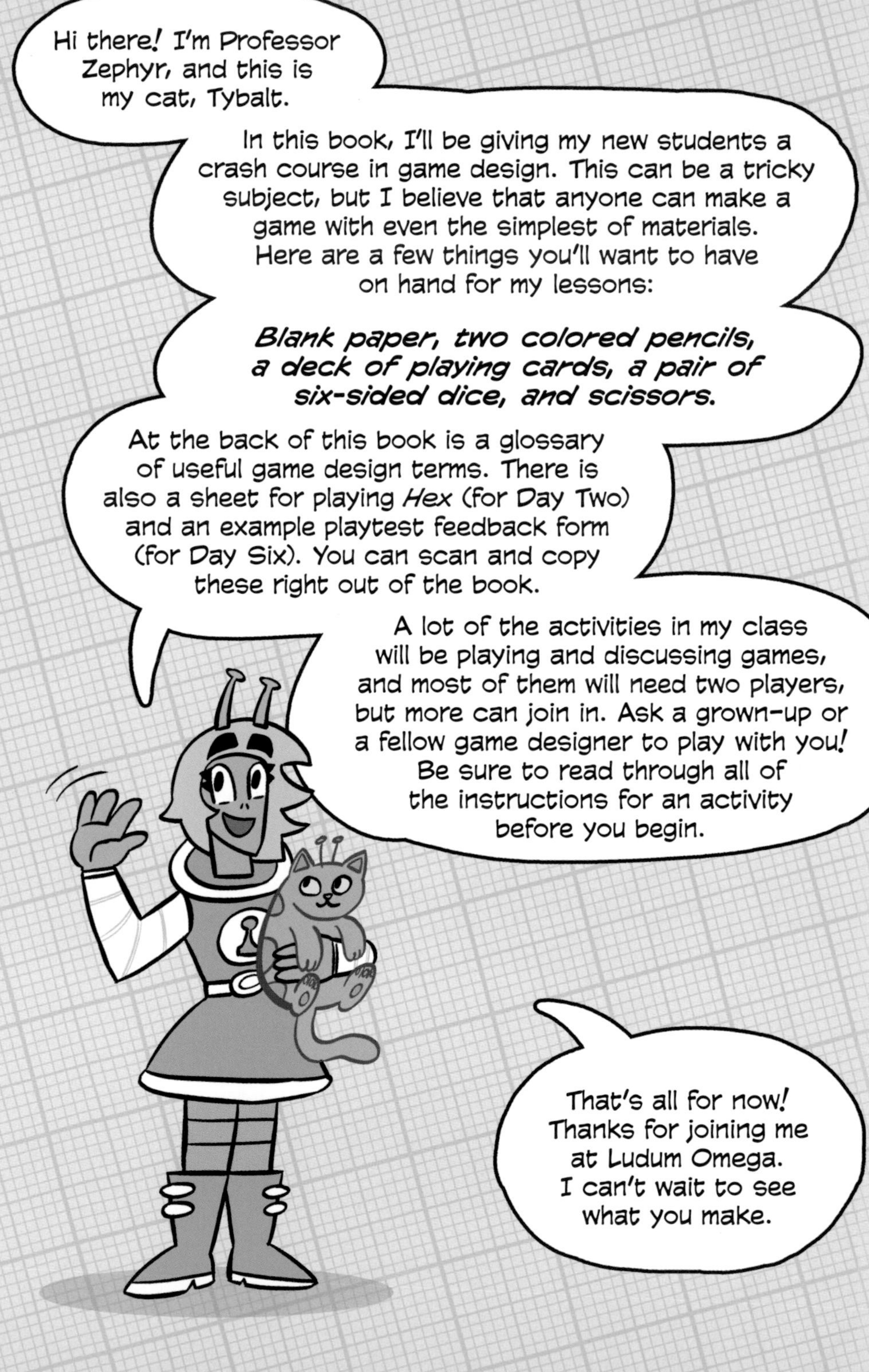
Hi there! I'm Professor Zephyr, and this is my cat, Tybalt.
In this book, I'll be giving my new students a crash course in game design. This can be a tricky subject, but I believe that anyone can make a game with even the simplest of materials. Here are a few things you'll want to have on hand for my lessons:
Blank paper, two colored pencils, a deck of playing cards, a pair of six-sided dice, and scissors.
At the back of this book is a glossary of useful game design terms. There is also a sheet for playing *Hex* (for Day Two) and an example playtest feedback form (for Day Six). You can scan and copy these right out of the book.
A lot of the activities in my class will be playing and discussing games, and most of them will need two players, but more can join in. Ask a grown-up or a fellow game designer to play with you! Be sure to read through all of the instructions for an activity before you begin.
That's all for now! Thanks for joining me at Ludum Omega. I can't wait to see what you make.

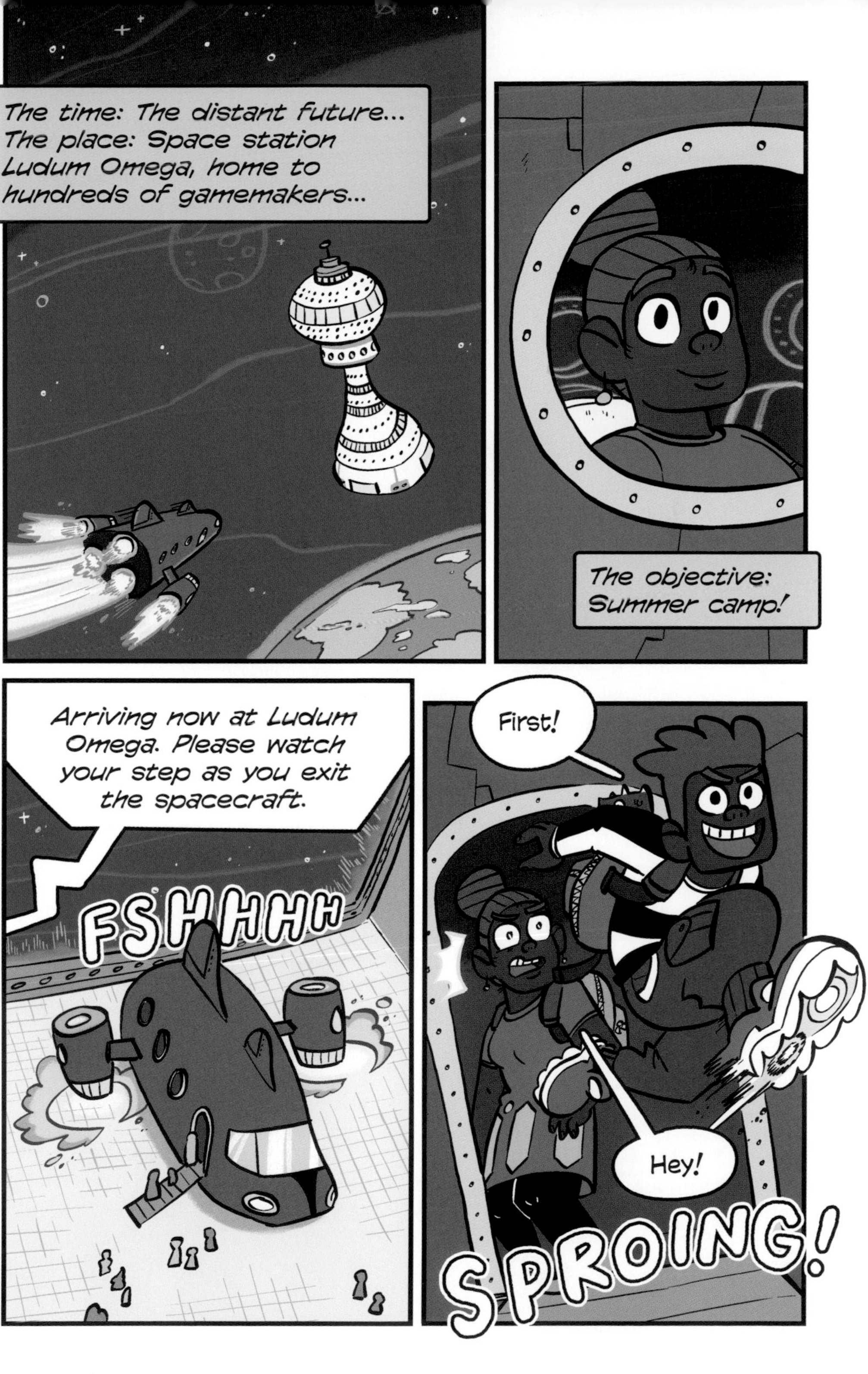
The time: The distant future...
The place: Space station Ludum Omega, home to hundreds of gamemakers...
The objective: Summer camp!
Arriving now at Ludum Omega. Please watch your step as you exit the spacecraft.
FSHHHHH
First!
Hey!
SPROING!

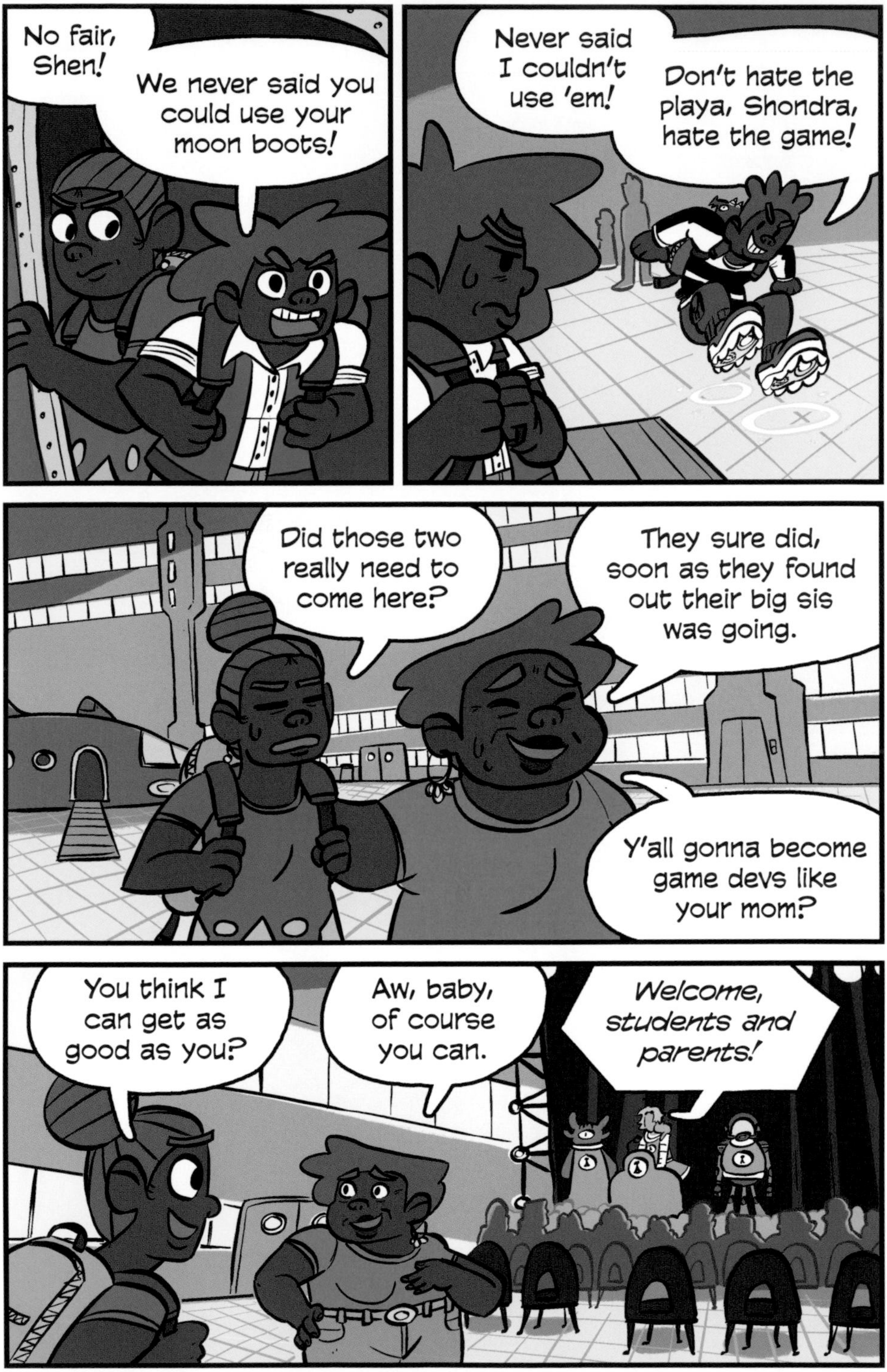
No fair, Shen!
We never said you could use your moon boots!
Never said I couldn't use 'em!
Don't hate the playa, Shondra, hate the game!
Did those two really need to come here?
They sure did, soon as they found out their big sis was going.
Y'all gonna become game devs like your mom?
You think I can get as good as you?
Aw, baby, of course you can.
Welcome, students and parents!

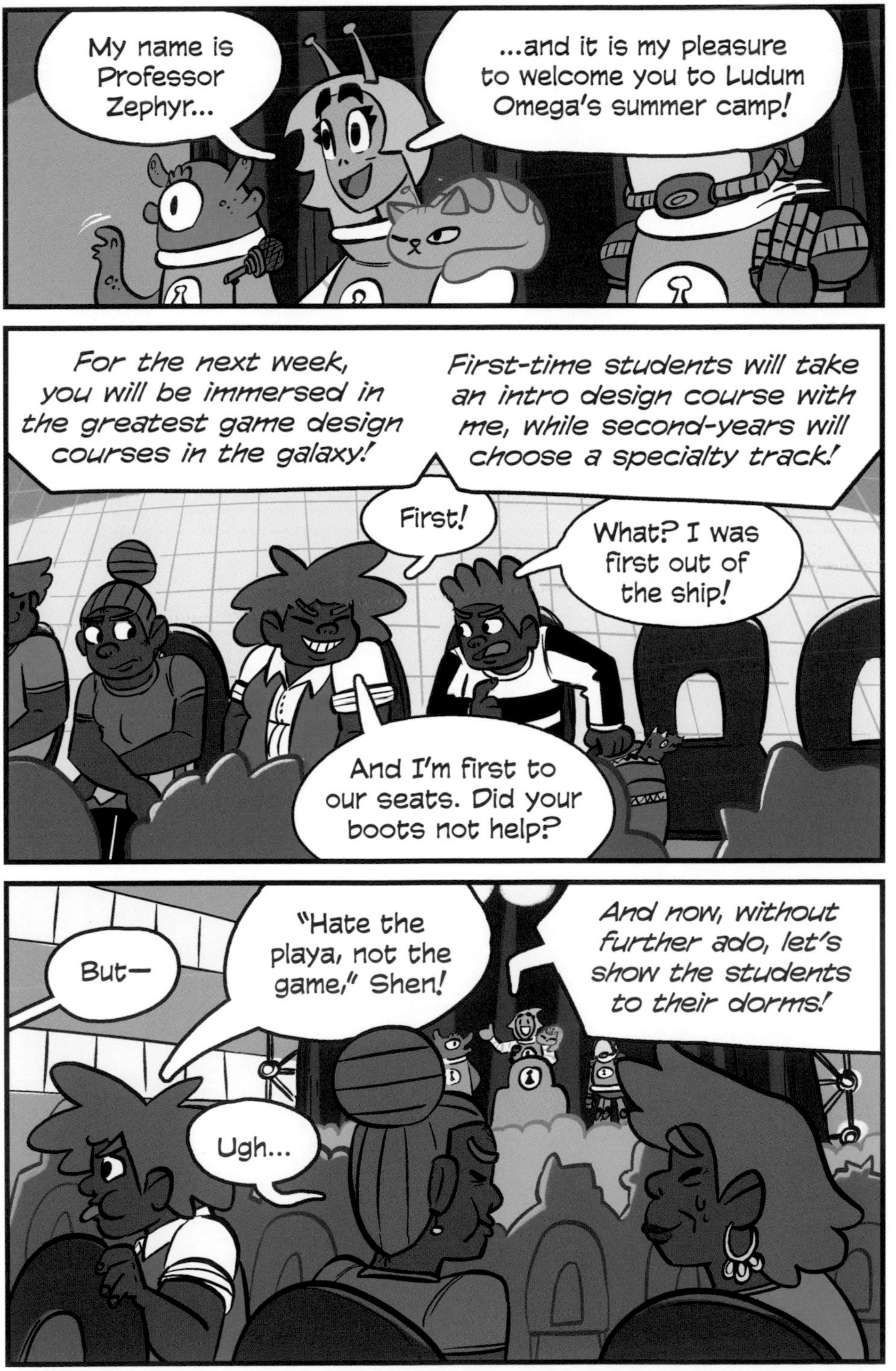
My name is Professor Zephyr...
...and it is my pleasure to welcome you to Ludum Omega's summer camp!
For the next week, you will be immersed in the greatest game design courses in the galaxy!
First-time students will take an intro design course with me, while second-years will choose a specialty track!
First!
What? I was first out of the ship!
And I'm first to our seats. Did your boots not help?
But—
"Hate the playa, not the game," Shen!
And now, without further ado, let's show the students to their dorms!
Ugh...

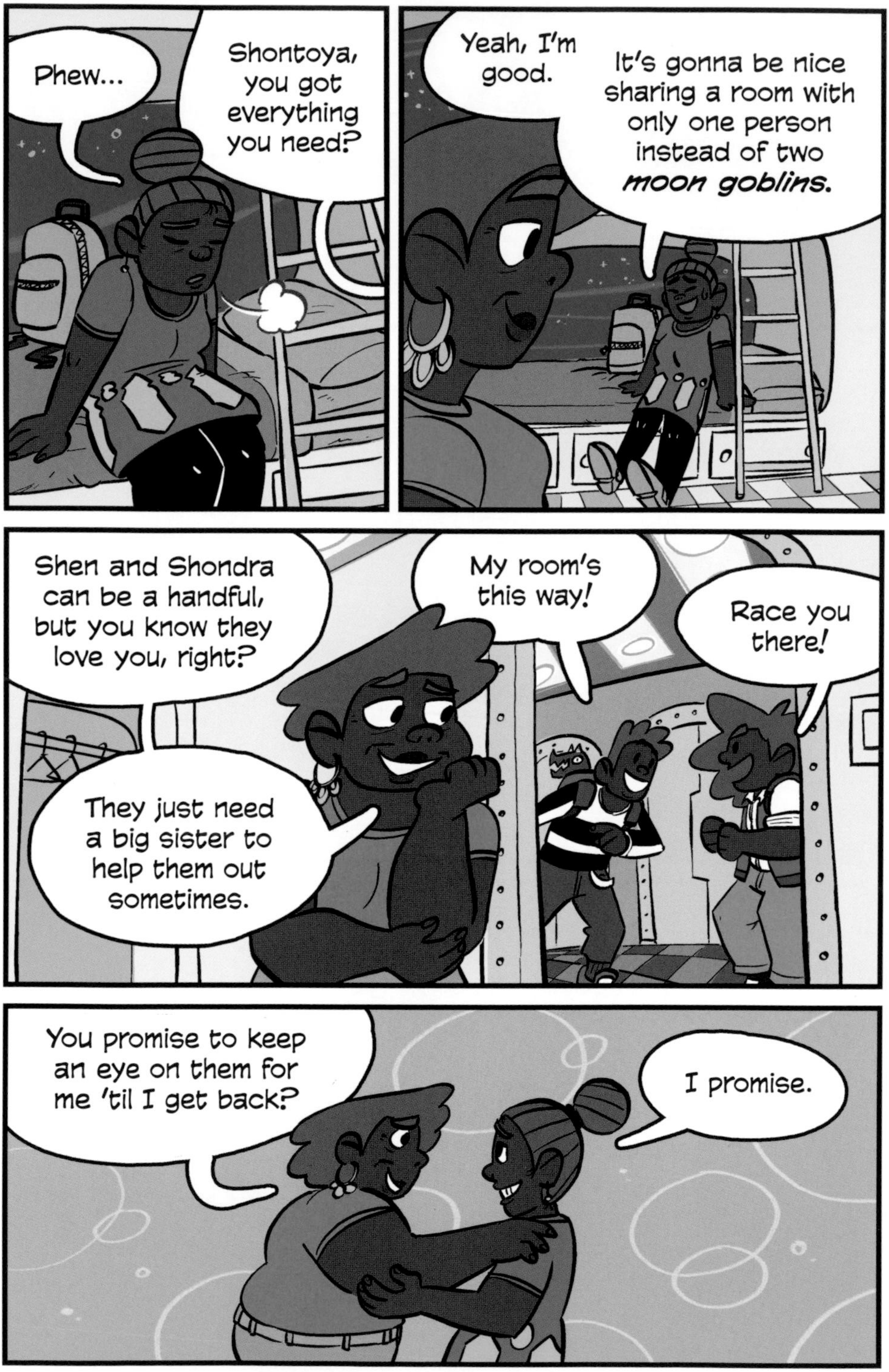
Phew...
Shontoya, you got everything you need?
Yeah, I'm good.
It's gonna be nice sharing a room with only one person instead of two ***moon goblins.***
Shen and Shondra can be a handful, but you know they love you, right?
They just need a big sister to help them out sometimes.
My room's this way!
Race you there!
You promise to keep an eye on them for me 'til I get back?
I promise.

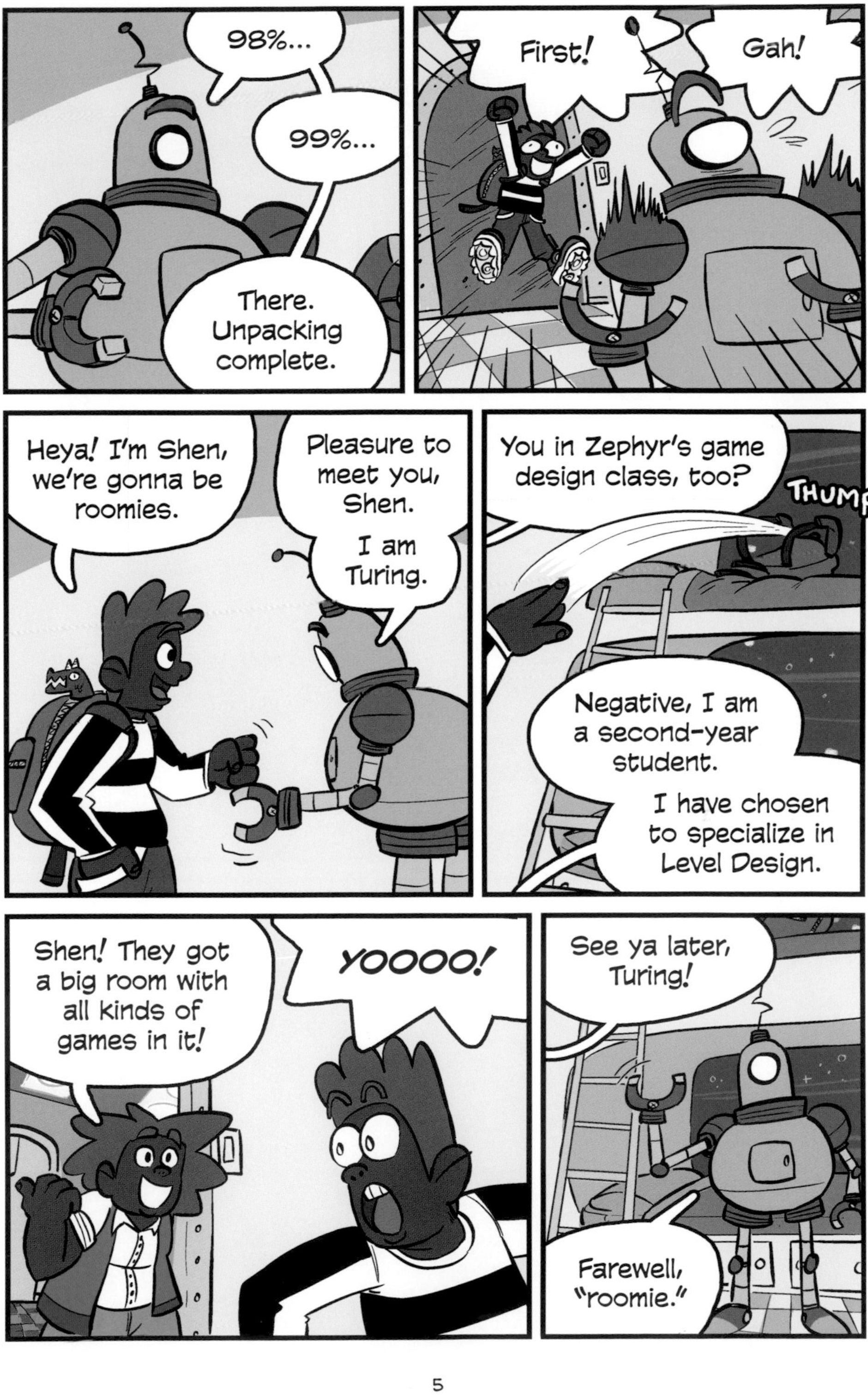
98%...
99%...
There. Unpacking complete.
First!
Gah!
Heya! I'm Shen, we're gonna be roomies.
Pleasure to meet you, Shen.
I am Turing.
You in Zephyr's game design class, too?
THUMP
Negative, I am a second-year student.
I have chosen to specialize in Level Design.
Shen! They got a big room with all kinds of games in it!
YOOOO!
See ya later, Turing!
Farewell, "roomie."

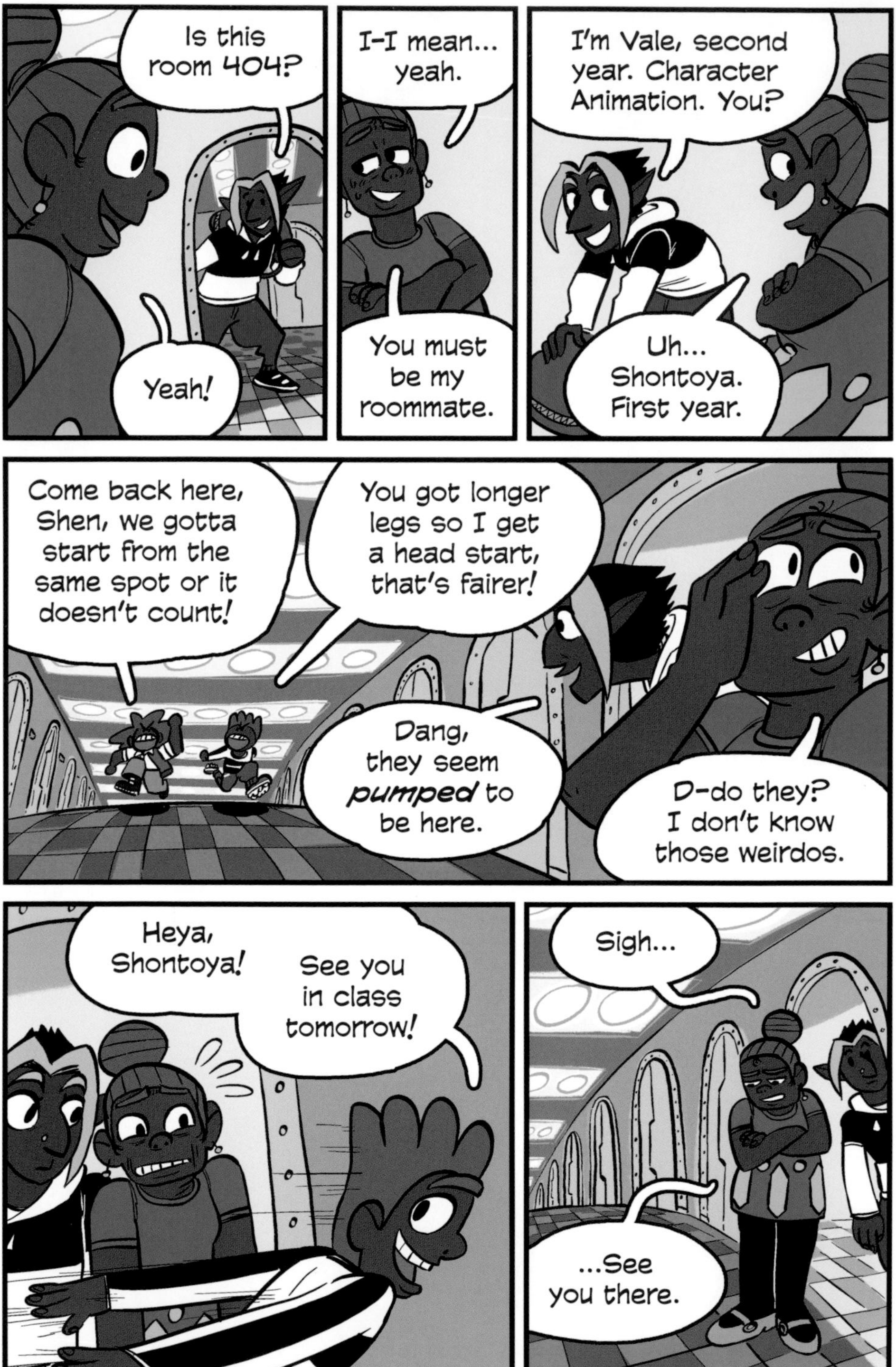
Is this room 404?
Yeah!
I-I mean... yeah.
You must be my roommate.
I'm Vale, second year. Character Animation. You?
Uh... Shontoya. First year.
Come back here, Shen, we gotta start from the same spot or it doesn't count!
You got longer legs so I get a head start, that's fairer!
Dang, they seem *pumped* to be here.
D-do they? I don't know those weirdos.
Heya, Shontoya!
See you in class tomorrow!
Sigh...
...See you there.

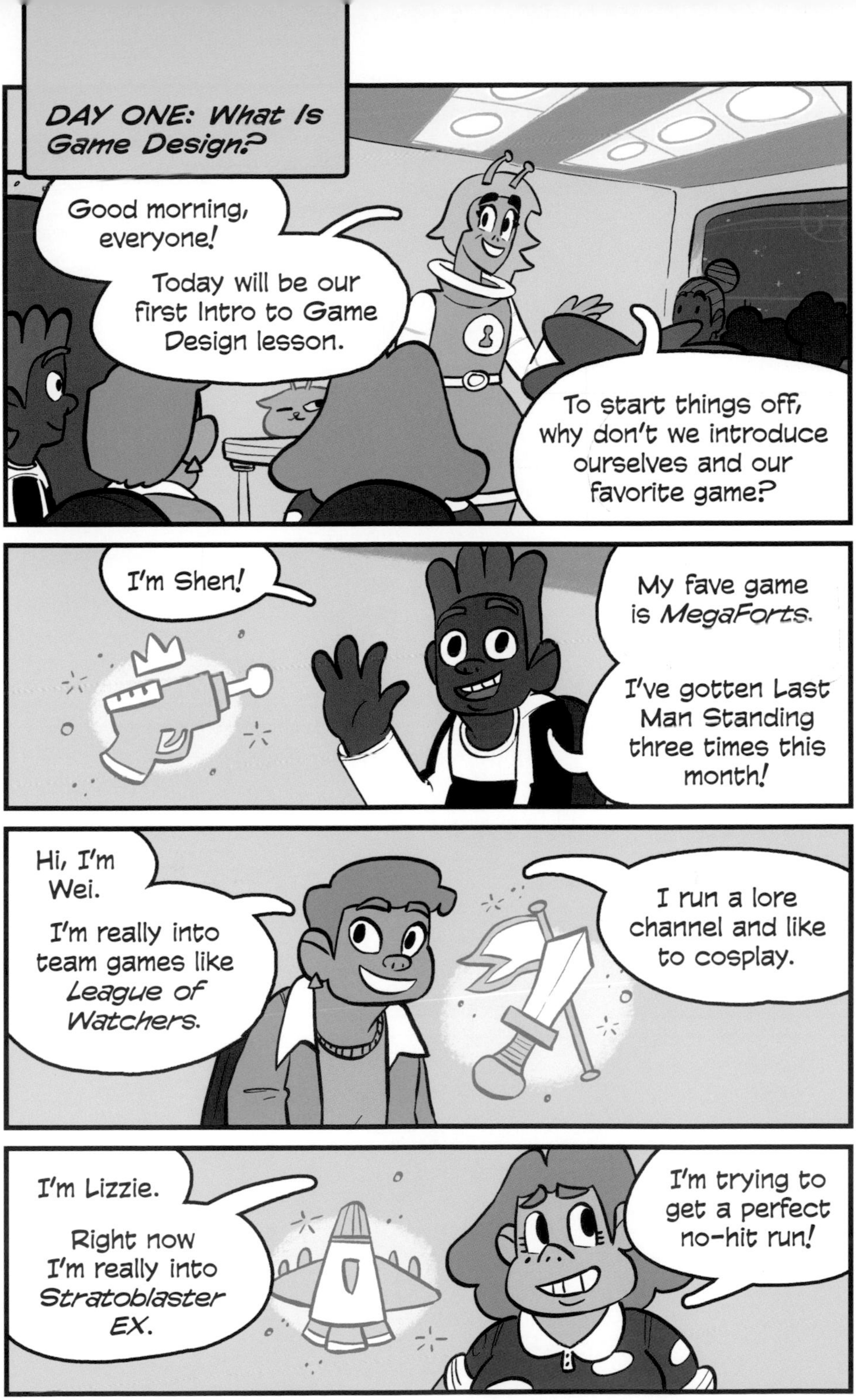
DAY ONE: What Is Game Design?
Good morning, everyone!
Today will be our first Intro to Game Design lesson.
To start things off, why don't we introduce ourselves and our favorite game?
I'm Shen!
My fave game is *MegaForts*.
I've gotten Last Man Standing three times this month!
Hi, I'm Wei.
I'm really into team games like *League of Watchers*.
I run a lore channel and like to cosplay.
I'm Lizzie.
Right now I'm really into *Stratoblaster EX*.
I'm trying to get a perfect no-hit run!

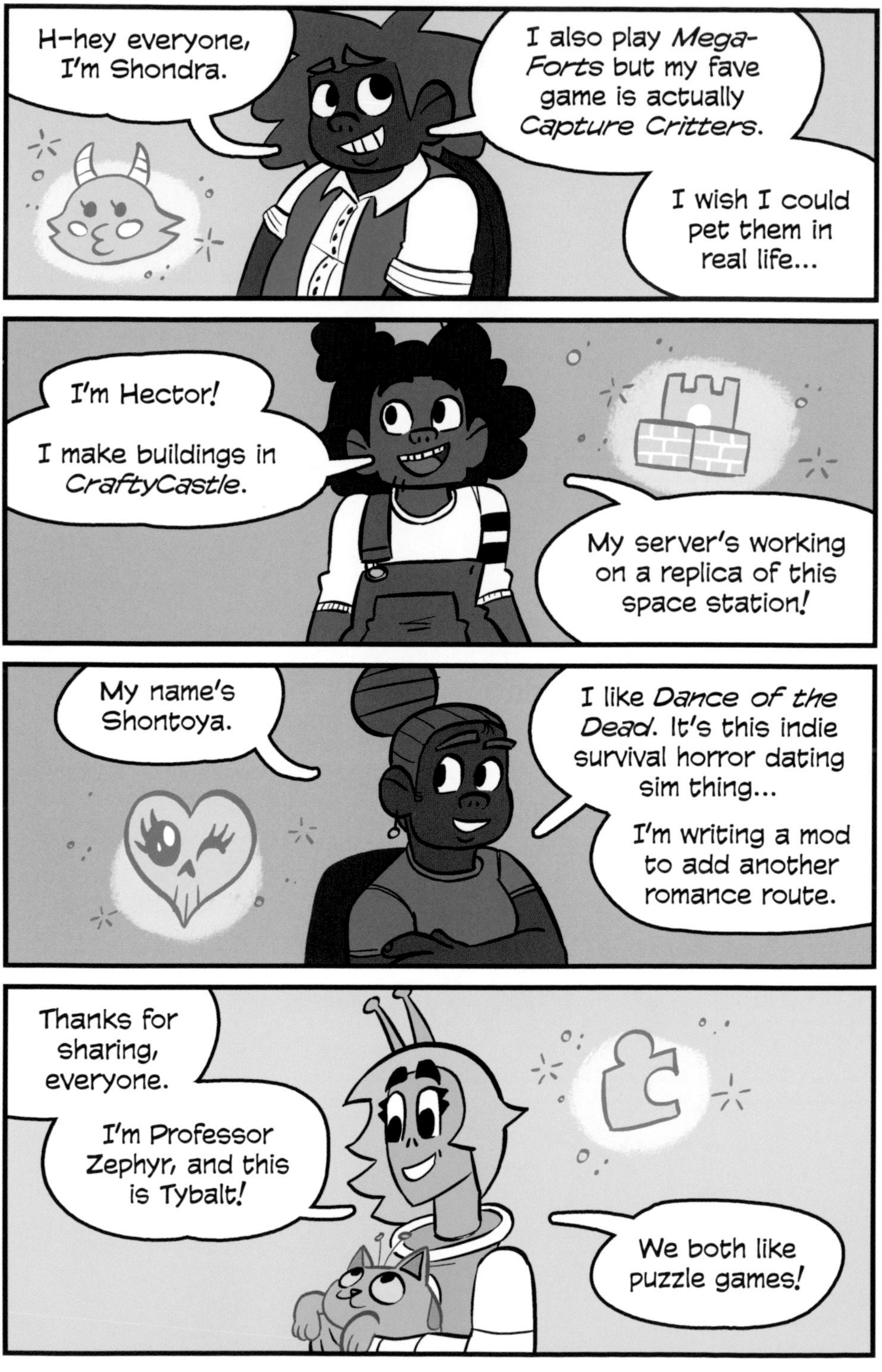
H-hey everyone, I'm Shondra.
I also play *Mega-Forts* but my fave game is actually *Capture Critters*.
I wish I could pet them in real life...
I'm Hector!
I make buildings in *CraftyCastle*.
My server's working on a replica of this space station!
My name's Shontoya.
I like *Dance of the Dead*. It's this indie survival horror dating sim thing...
I'm writing a mod to add another romance route.
Thanks for sharing, everyone.
I'm Professor Zephyr, and this is Tybalt!
We both like puzzle games!

10

Let's Play *Mind Meld!*

Players:	Materials:	Time to play:
2+	None	5 minutes

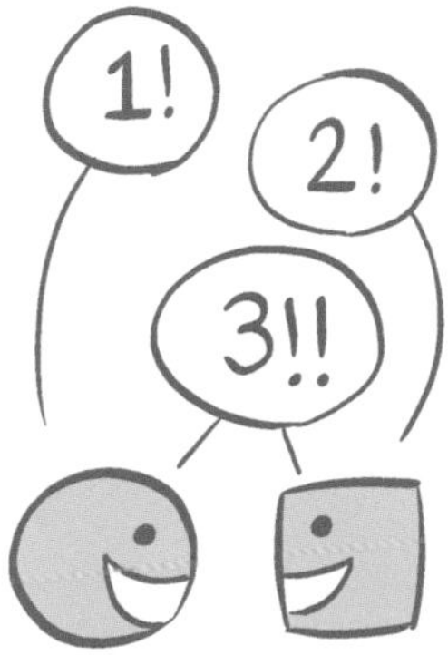
1!
2!
3!!

1. Two players stand face-to-face. They count to three, with player A saying "one," player B saying "two," and both players saying "three."

2. After the players say "three," they both simultaneously say any noun they can think of.

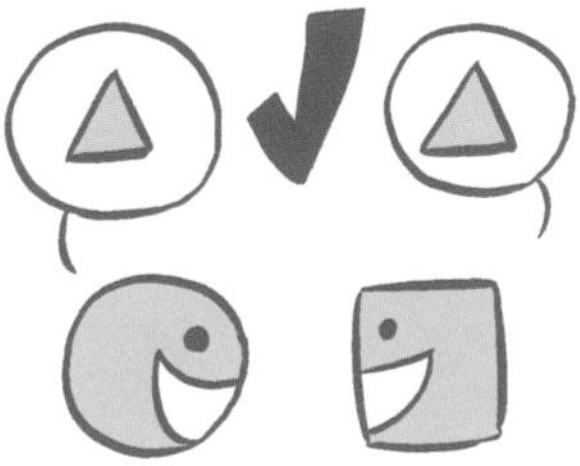

3. If both players say the same noun, they both win! If not, they begin a new round and count down again. Play continues until both players say the same noun.

4. Players cannot say the same word twice (or a word that's too similar). Players cannot discuss what words they should say before counting down.

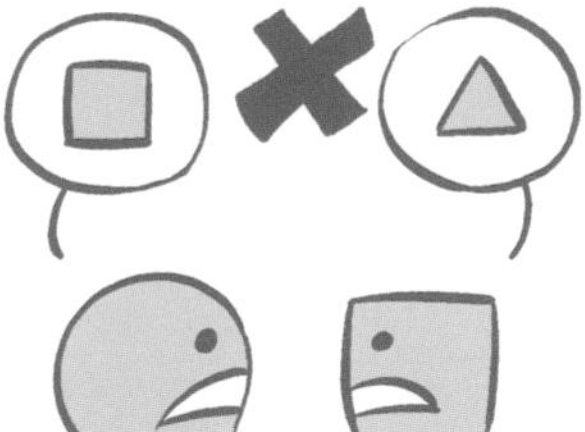

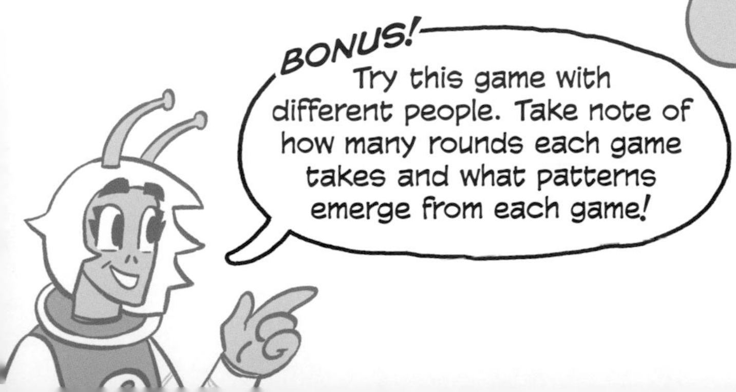
BONUS!
Try this game with different people. Take note of how many rounds each game takes and what patterns emerge from each game!

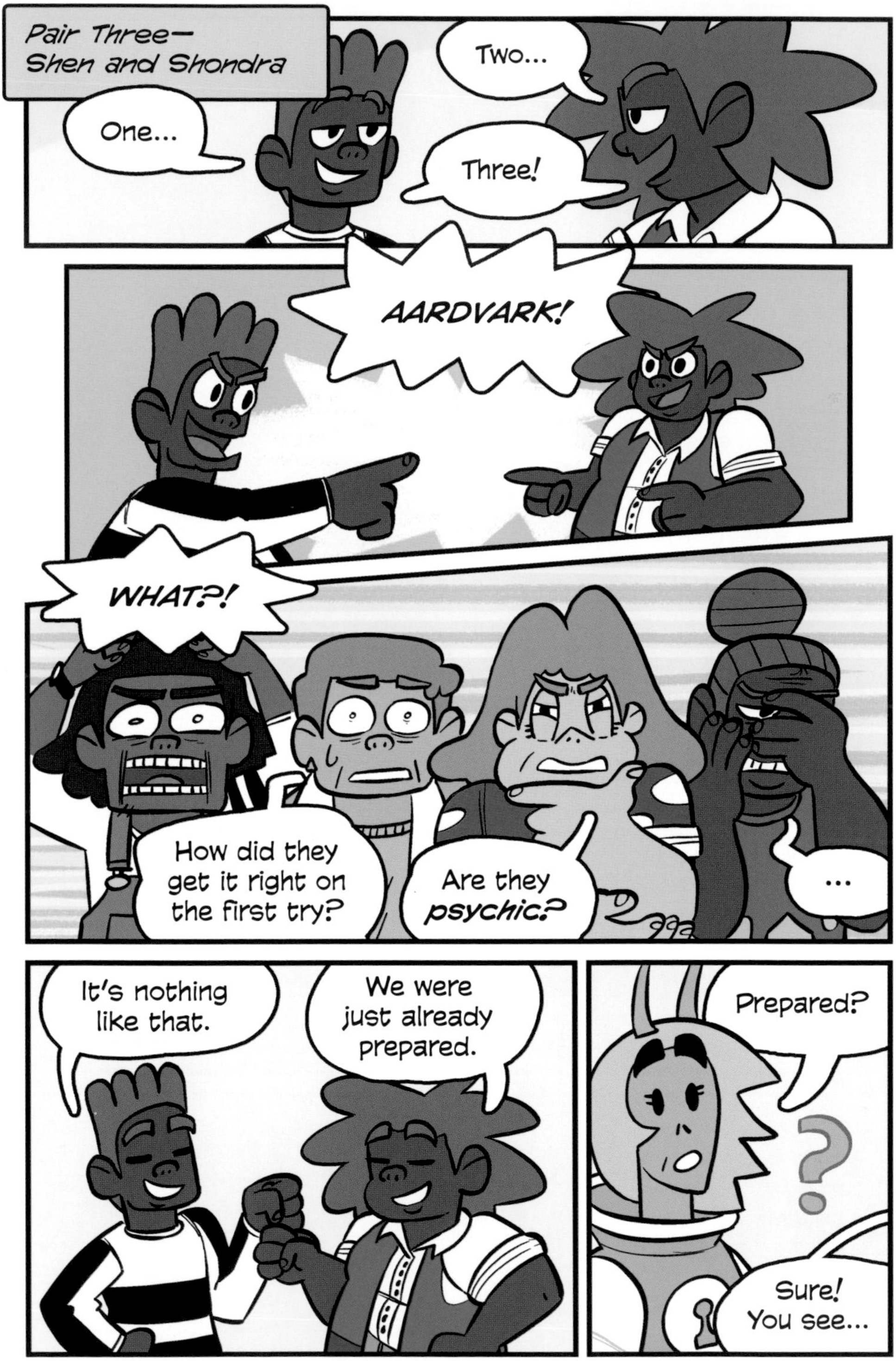
Pair Three—
Shen and Shondra
One...
Two...
Three!
AARDVARK!
WHAT?!
How did they get it right on the first try?
Are they *psychic?*
...
It's nothing like that.
We were just already prepared.
Prepared?
?
Sure! You see...

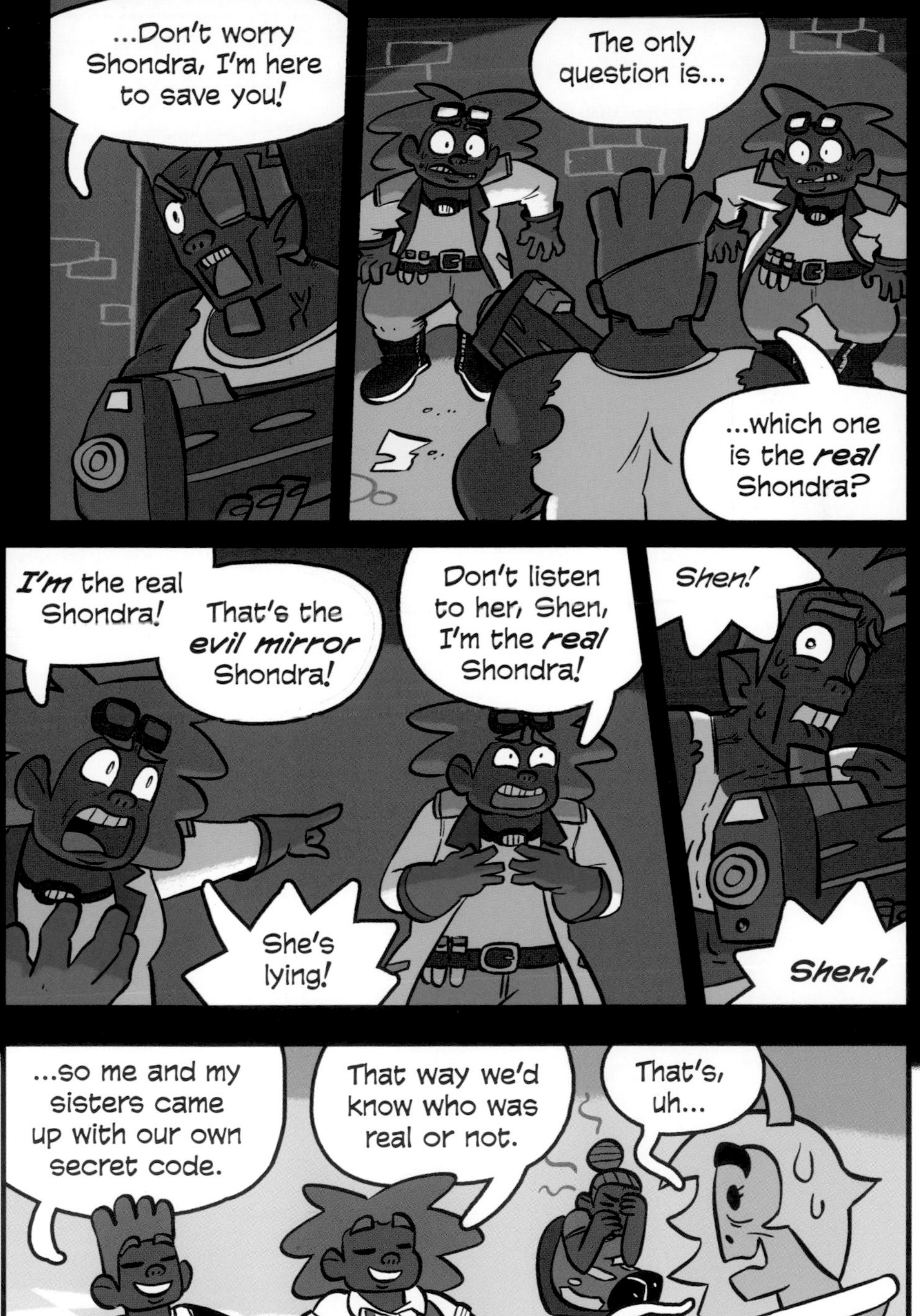
...Don't worry Shondra, I'm here to save you!
The only question is...
...which one is the *real* Shondra?
I'm the real Shondra!
That's the *evil mirror* Shondra!
She's lying!
Don't listen to her, Shen, I'm the *real* Shondra!
Shen!
Shen!
...so me and my sisters came up with our own secret code.
That way we'd know who was real or not.
That's, uh...
...very thoughtful.

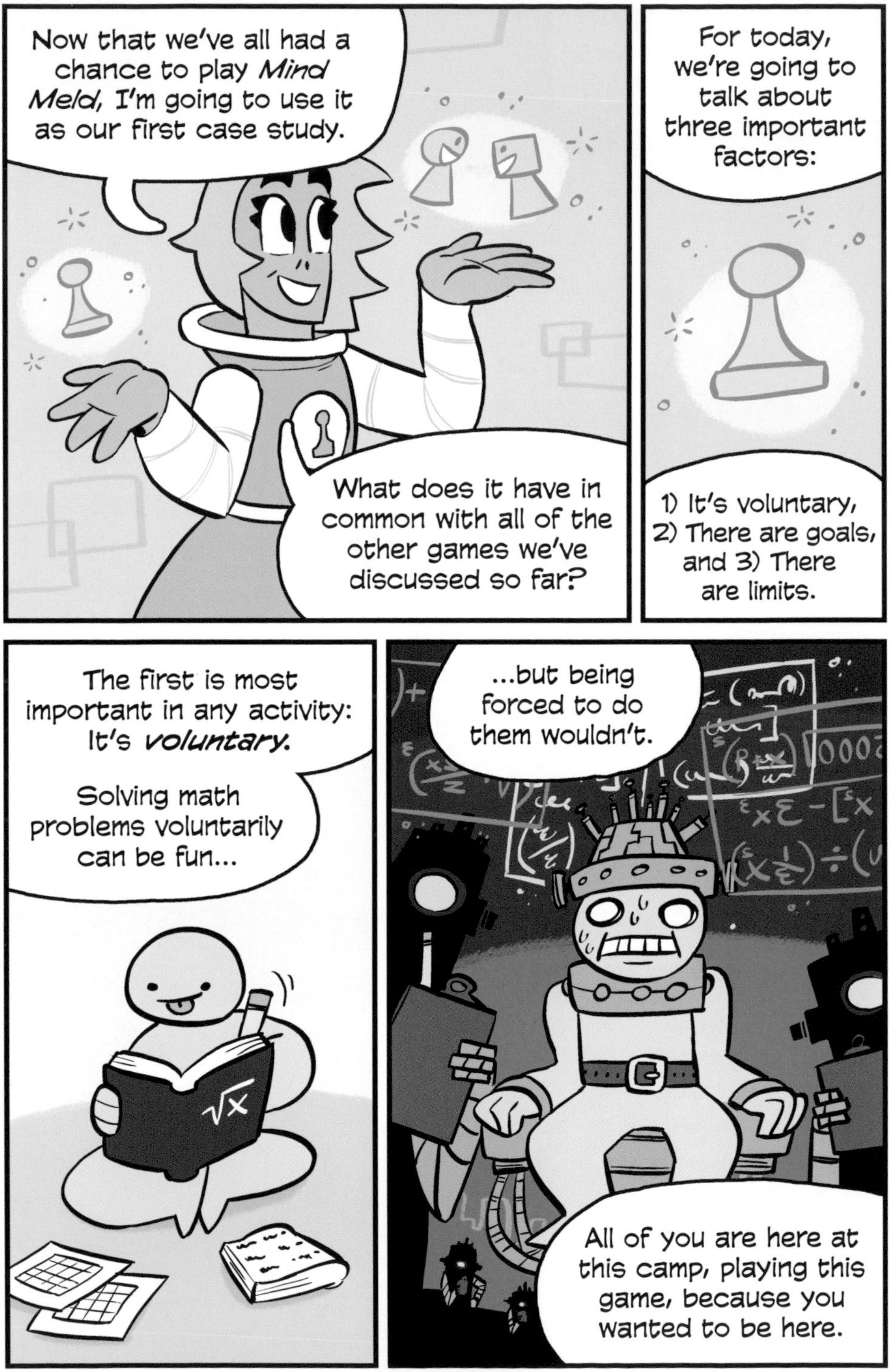
Now that we've all had a chance to play *Mind Meld,* I'm going to use it as our first case study.
What does it have in common with all of the other games we've discussed so far?
For today, we're going to talk about three important factors:
1) It's voluntary, 2) There are goals, and 3) There are limits.
The first is most important in any activity: It's ***voluntary.***
Solving math problems voluntarily can be fun...
...but being forced to do them wouldn't.
All of you are here at this camp, playing this game, because you wanted to be here.

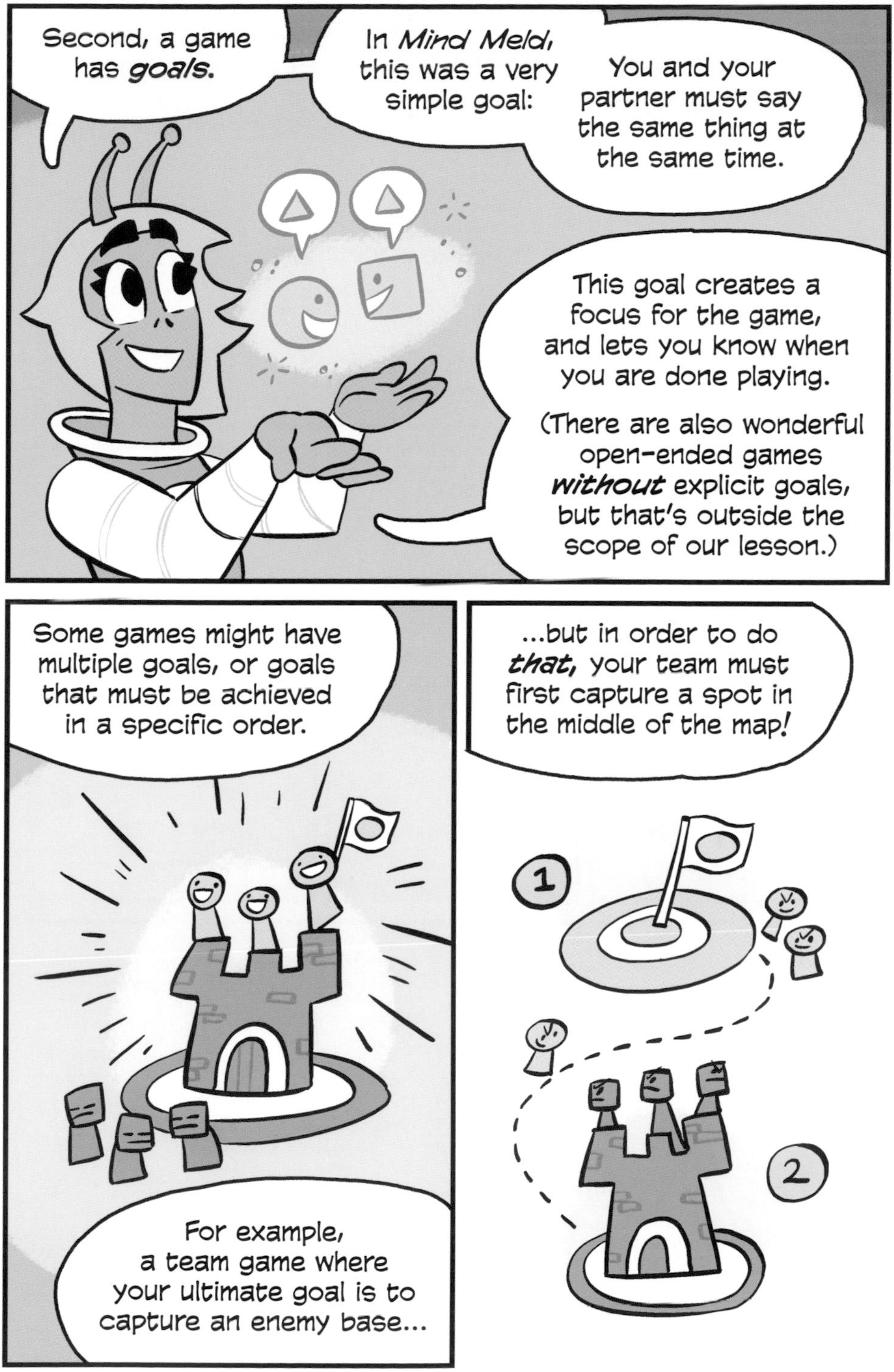
Second, a game has *goals.*
In *Mind Meld,* this was a very simple goal:
You and your partner must say the same thing at the same time.
This goal creates a focus for the game, and lets you know when you are done playing.
(There are also wonderful open-ended games ***without*** explicit goals, but that's outside the scope of our lesson.)
Some games might have multiple goals, or goals that must be achieved in a specific order.
For example, a team game where your ultimate goal is to capture an enemy base...
...but in order to do ***that,*** your team must first capture a spot in the middle of the map!
1
2

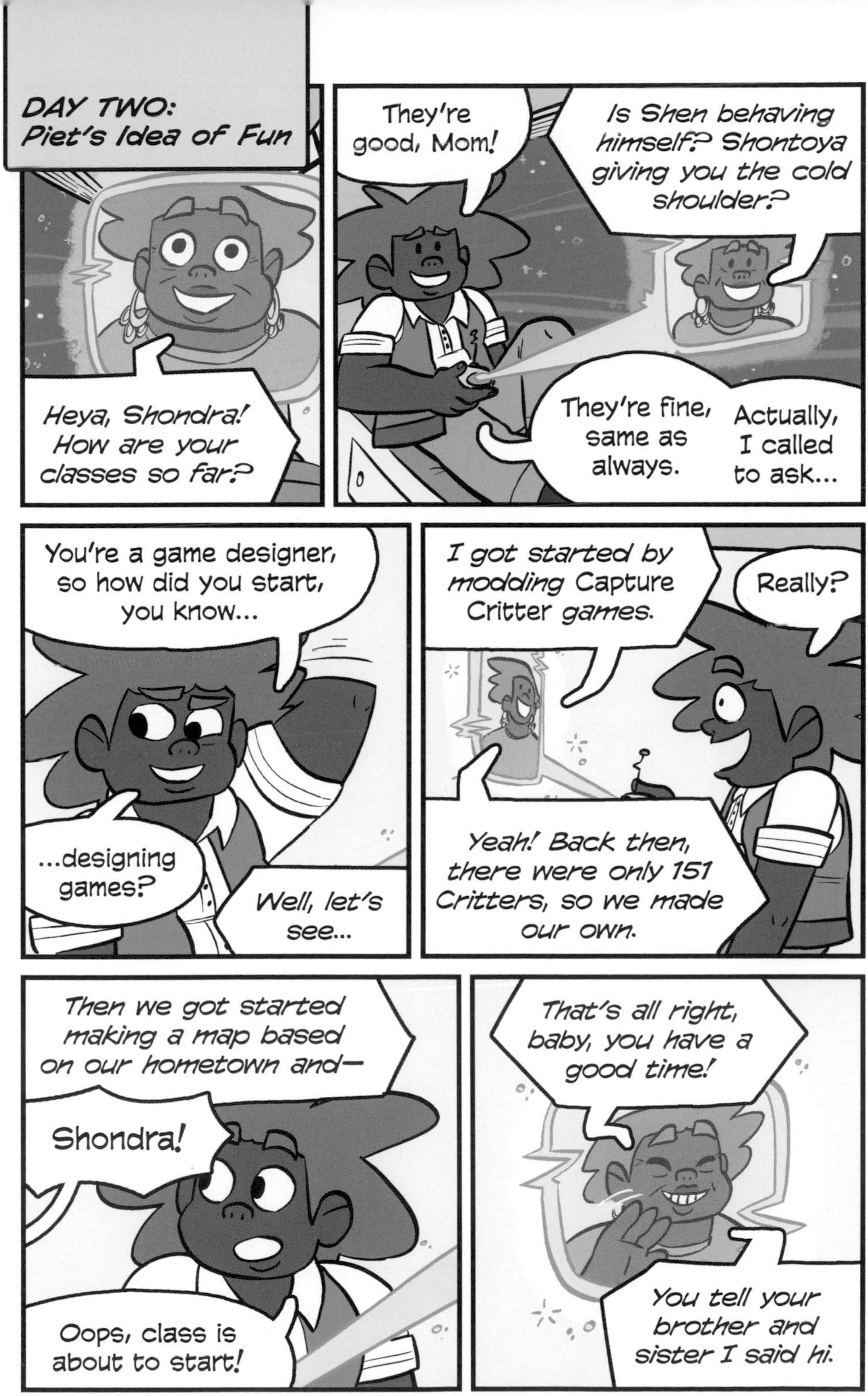

DAY TWO:
Piet's Idea of Fun
Heya, Shondra! How are your classes so far?
They're good, Mom!
Is Shen behaving himself? Shontoya giving you the cold shoulder?
They're fine, same as always.
Actually, I called to ask...
You're a game designer, so how did you start, you know...
...designing games?
Well, let's see...
I got started by modding Capture Critter games.
Really?
Yeah! Back then, there were only 151 Critters, so we made our own.
Then we got started making a map based on our hometown and—
Shondra!
Oops, class is about to start!
That's all right, baby, you have a good time!
You tell your brother and sister I said hi.

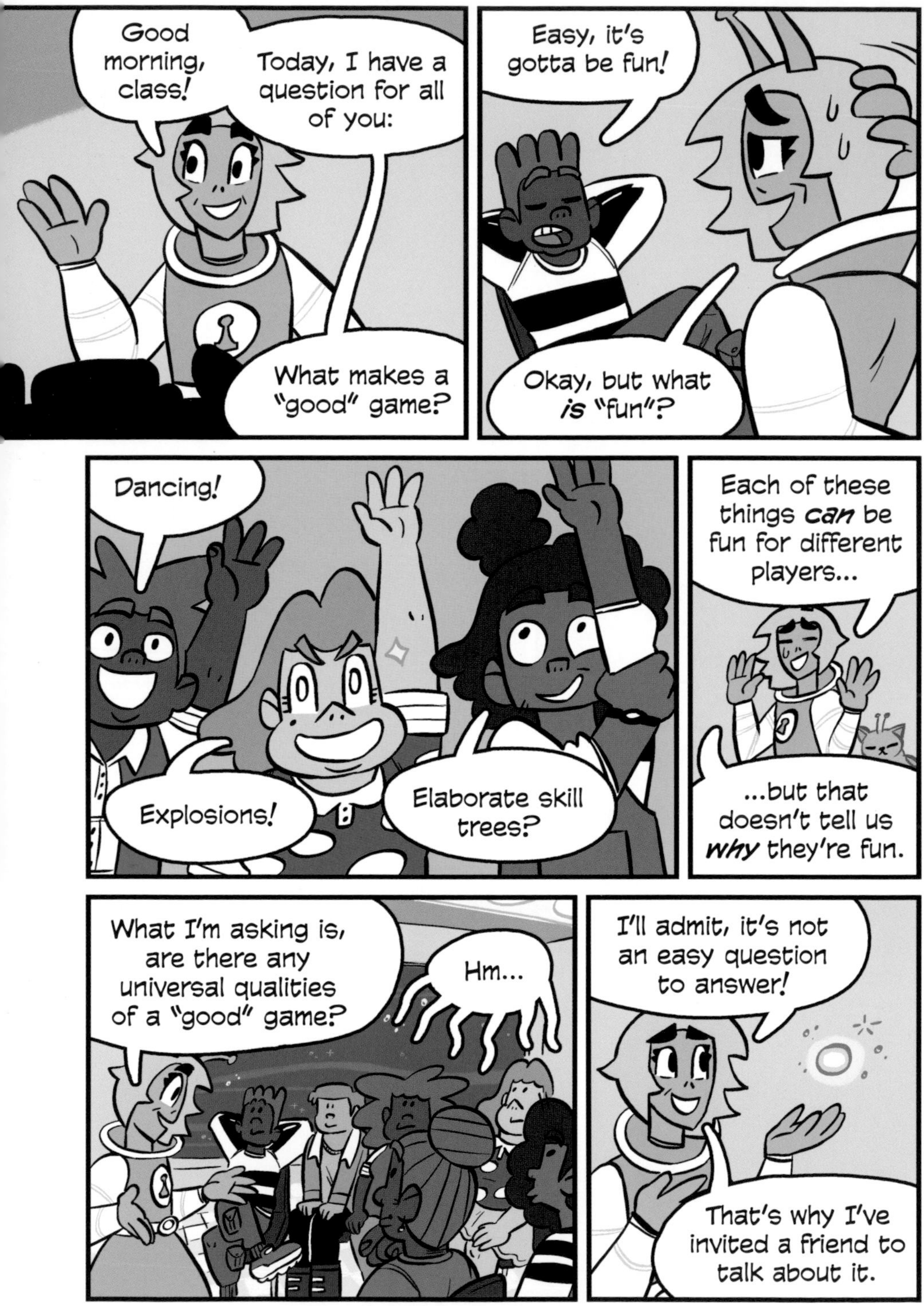
Good morning, class!
Today, I have a question for all of you:
What makes a "good" game?
Easy, it's gotta be fun!
Okay, but what *is* "fun"?
Dancing!
Explosions!
Elaborate skill trees?
Each of these things *can* be fun for different players...
...but that doesn't tell us *why* they're fun.
What I'm asking is, are there any universal qualities of a "good" game?
Hm...
I'll admit, it's not an easy question to answer!
That's why I've invited a friend to talk about it.

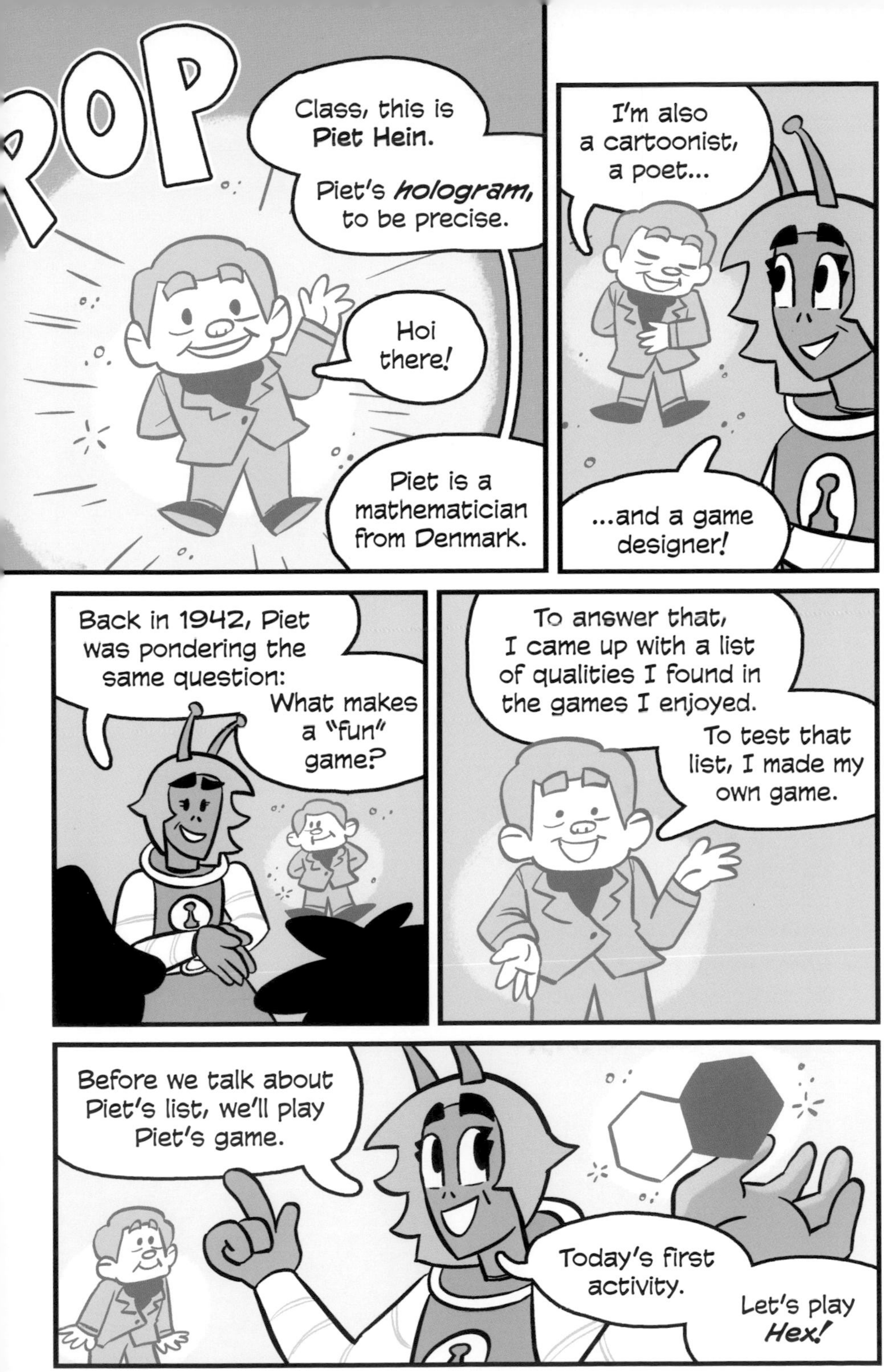
POP
Class, this is **Piet Hein.**
Piet's ***hologram,*** to be precise.
Hoi there!
Piet is a mathematician from Denmark.
I'm also a cartoonist, a poet...
...and a game designer!
Back in 1942, Piet was pondering the same question:
What makes a "fun" game?
To answer that, I came up with a list of qualities I found in the games I enjoyed.
To test that list, I made my own game.
Before we talk about Piet's list, we'll play Piet's game.
Today's first activity.
Let's play ***Hex!***

Let's Play *Hex!*

Players: 2

Materials: 2 different colored pencils, printout of *Hex* game board

Time to play: 5–10 minutes

1. Copy and print the *Hex* template on page 122 to make your game board! Each player colors two opposite sides of the board with their pencil.

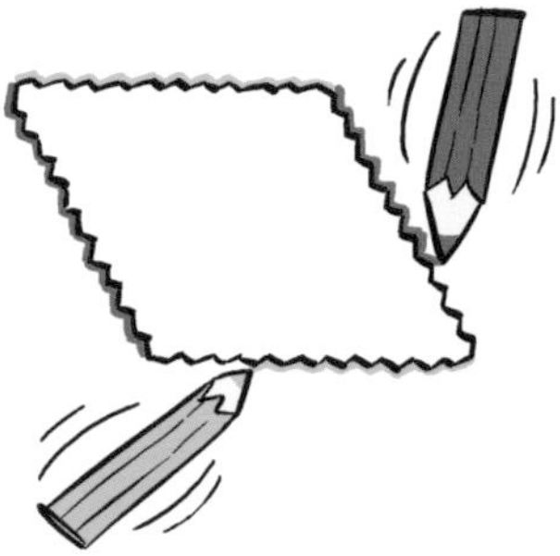

2. Flip a coin or play *rock-paper-scissors* to decide who goes first.

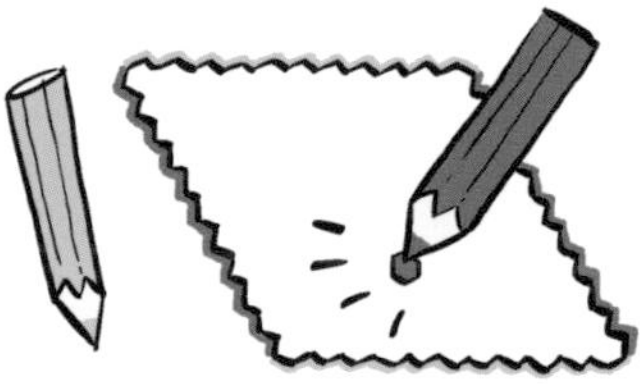

3. Players take turns coloring in one empty space on the board to claim it. When you color in a space, it becomes your territory!

   (Keep in mind that you do not have to choose spaces near ones you've already claimed!)

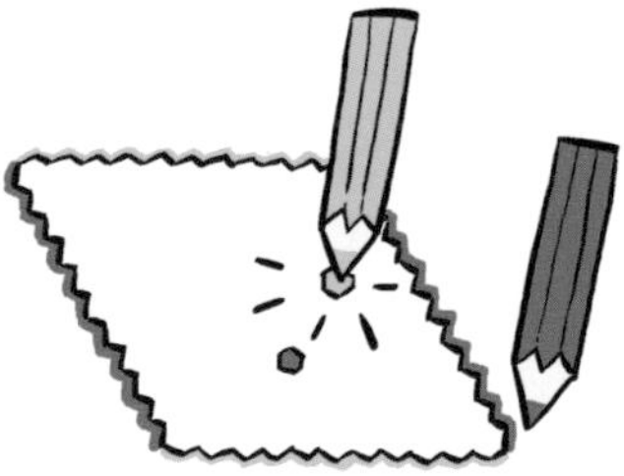

4. The first player to color a line connecting their two sides is the winner!

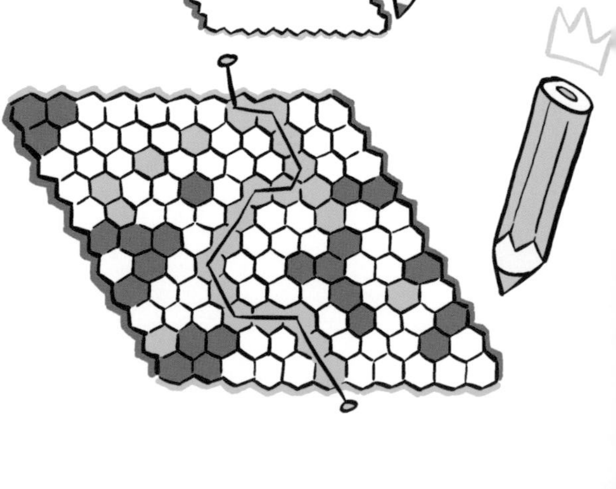

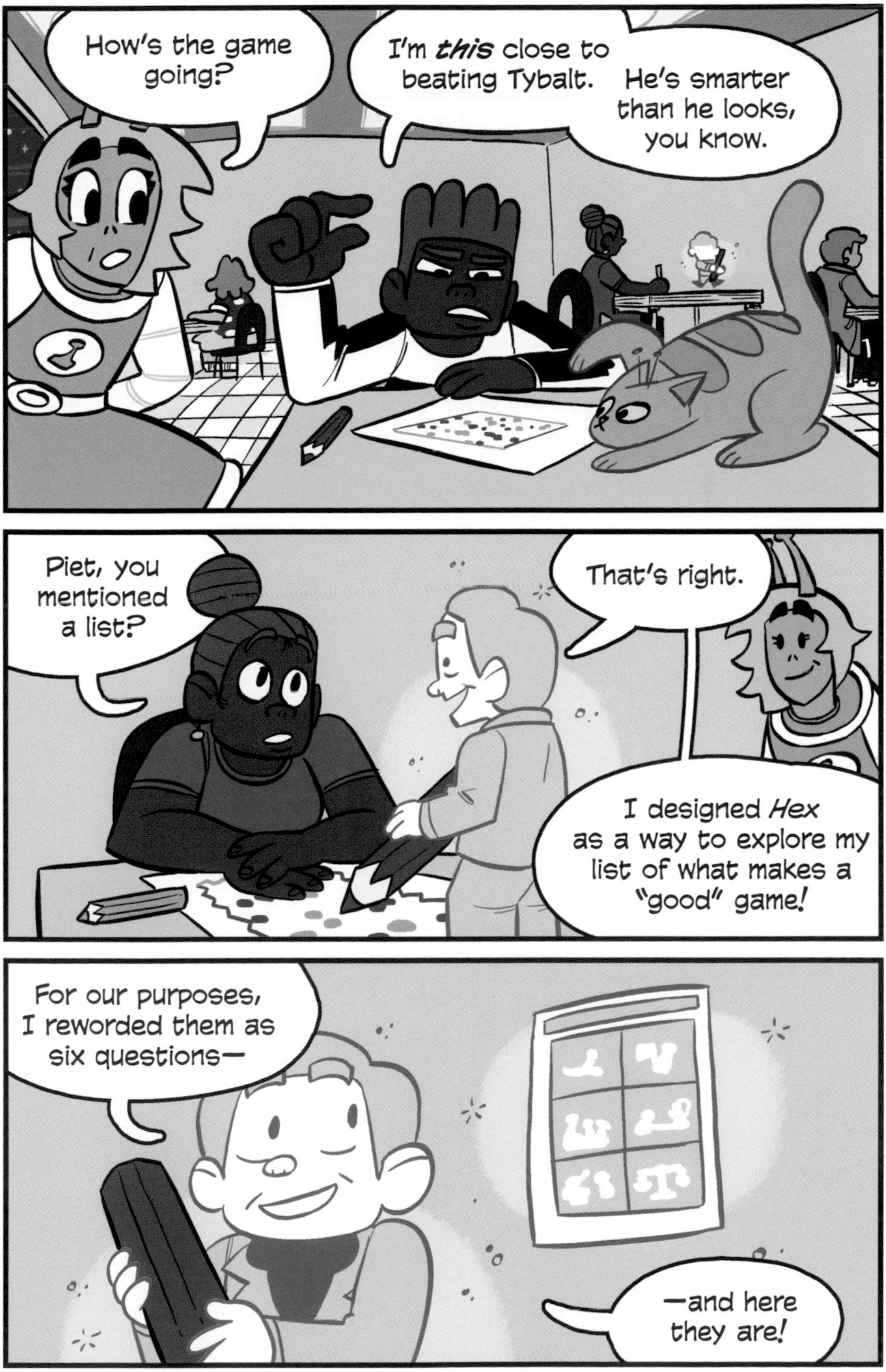
How's the game going?
I'm *this* close to beating Tybalt.
He's smarter than he looks, you know.
Piet, you mentioned a list?
That's right.
I designed *Hex* as a way to explore my list of what makes a "good" game!
For our purposes, I reworded them as six questions—
—and here they are!

33

Craige Schensted and Charles Titus created *Y*,
a game that was derived from Hex.

Make a New Game from *Hex!*

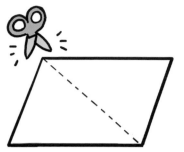

1. Create a *Y* board. (Actually, two!)
   Take a copy of the board on page
   122 and cut it in half as shown.

2. To win a game of *Y*, a player must
   connect all three sides of the
   board. (A corner space can count
   as either side.) Play a few games.
   How does it feel compared
   to *Hex?*

3. Play a game of *Hex*
   or *Y* with any one of
   these rule changes:

   a. Players can only
   choose a space
   next to one they
   have already
   claimed.

   b. There are
   spaces that
   nobody can use.

   c. Certain spaces
   allow you to claim
   an extra space
   on that turn.

   d. Play a "loser
   wins" variant:
   you only win if
   your *opponent*
   connects their
   sides.

You can also
come up with
your own!

As you make rule
changes and your
game evolves, your
version of *Hex* will
become more unique!

BONUS!
Try another person's
custom *Hex* game. How does
it feel playing this compared to
yours or to the normal
Hex game?

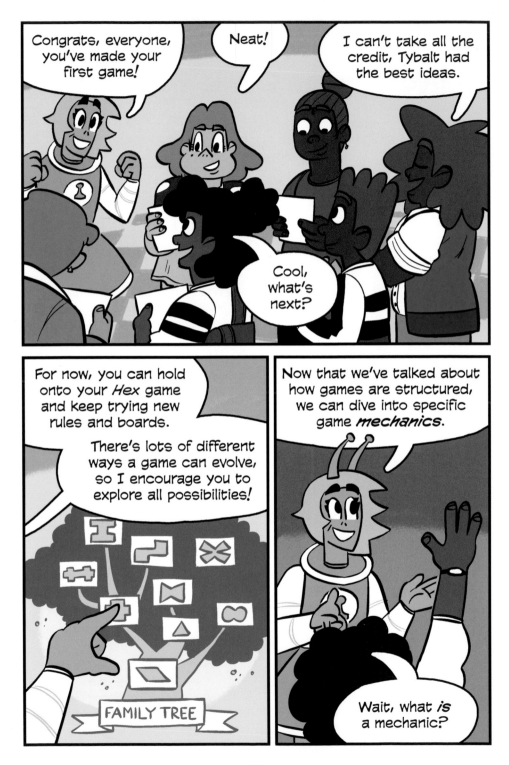

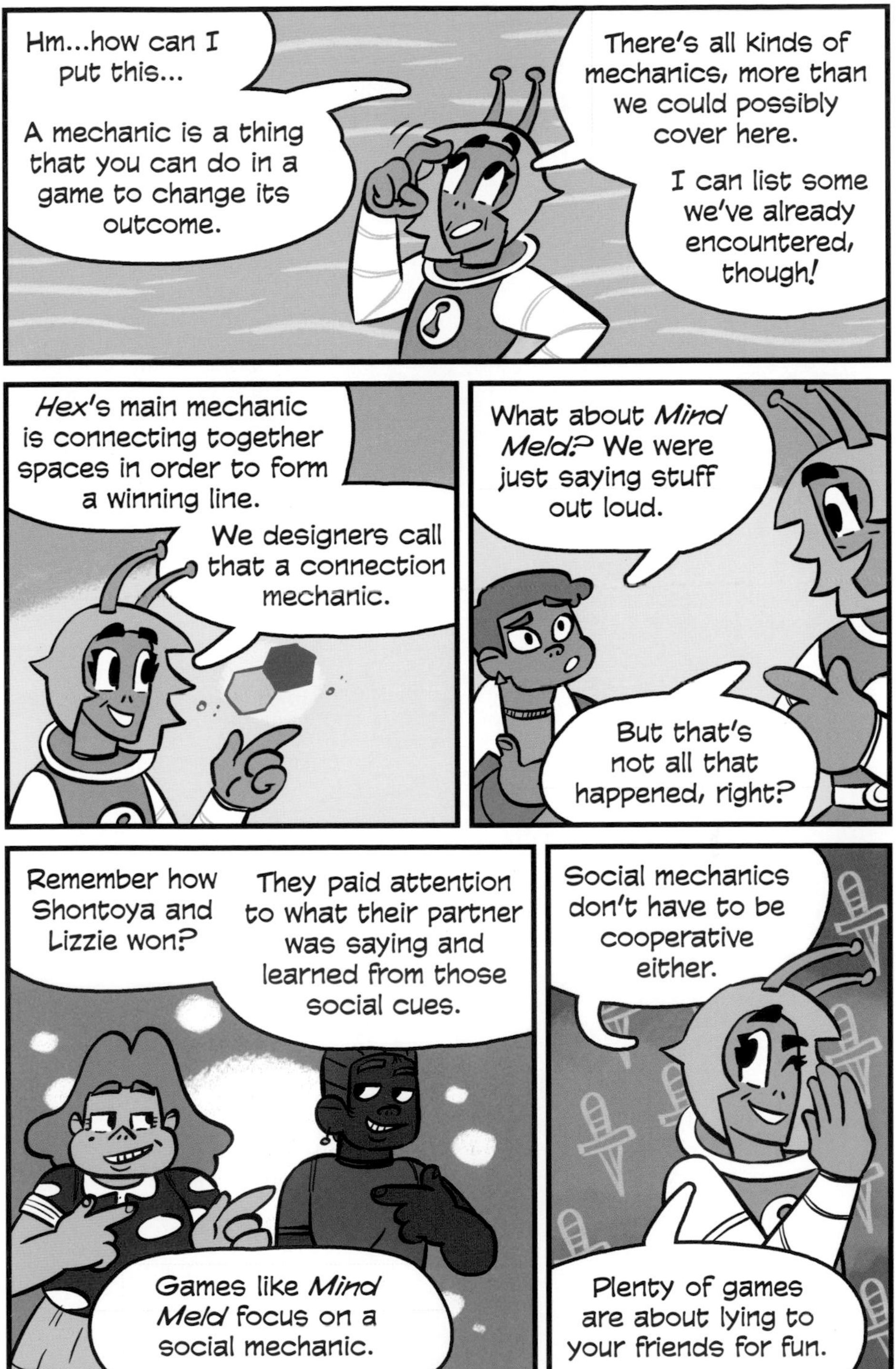
Hm...how can I put this...
A mechanic is a thing that you can do in a game to change its outcome.
There's all kinds of mechanics, more than we could possibly cover here.
I can list some we've already encountered, though!
Hex's main mechanic is connecting together spaces in order to form a winning line.
We designers call that a connection mechanic.
What about *Mind Meld*? We were just saying stuff out loud.
But that's not all that happened, right?
Remember how Shontoya and Lizzie won?
They paid attention to what their partner was saying and learned from those social cues.
Games like *Mind Meld* focus on a social mechanic.
Social mechanics don't have to be cooperative either.
Plenty of games are about lying to your friends for fun.

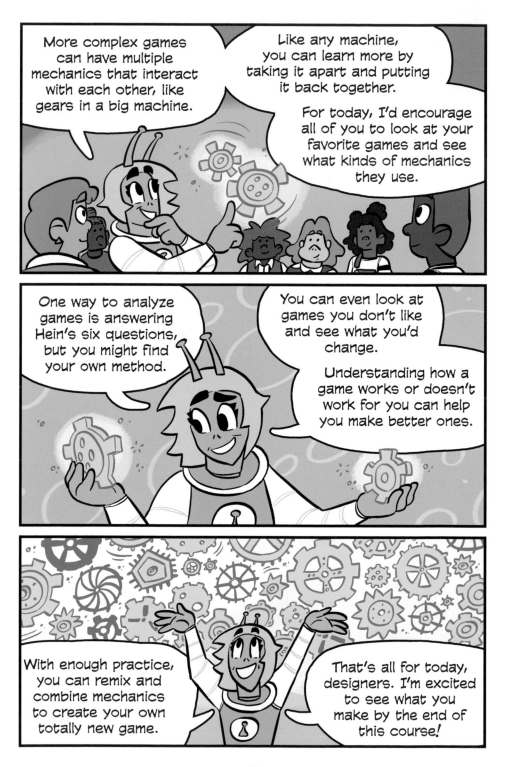

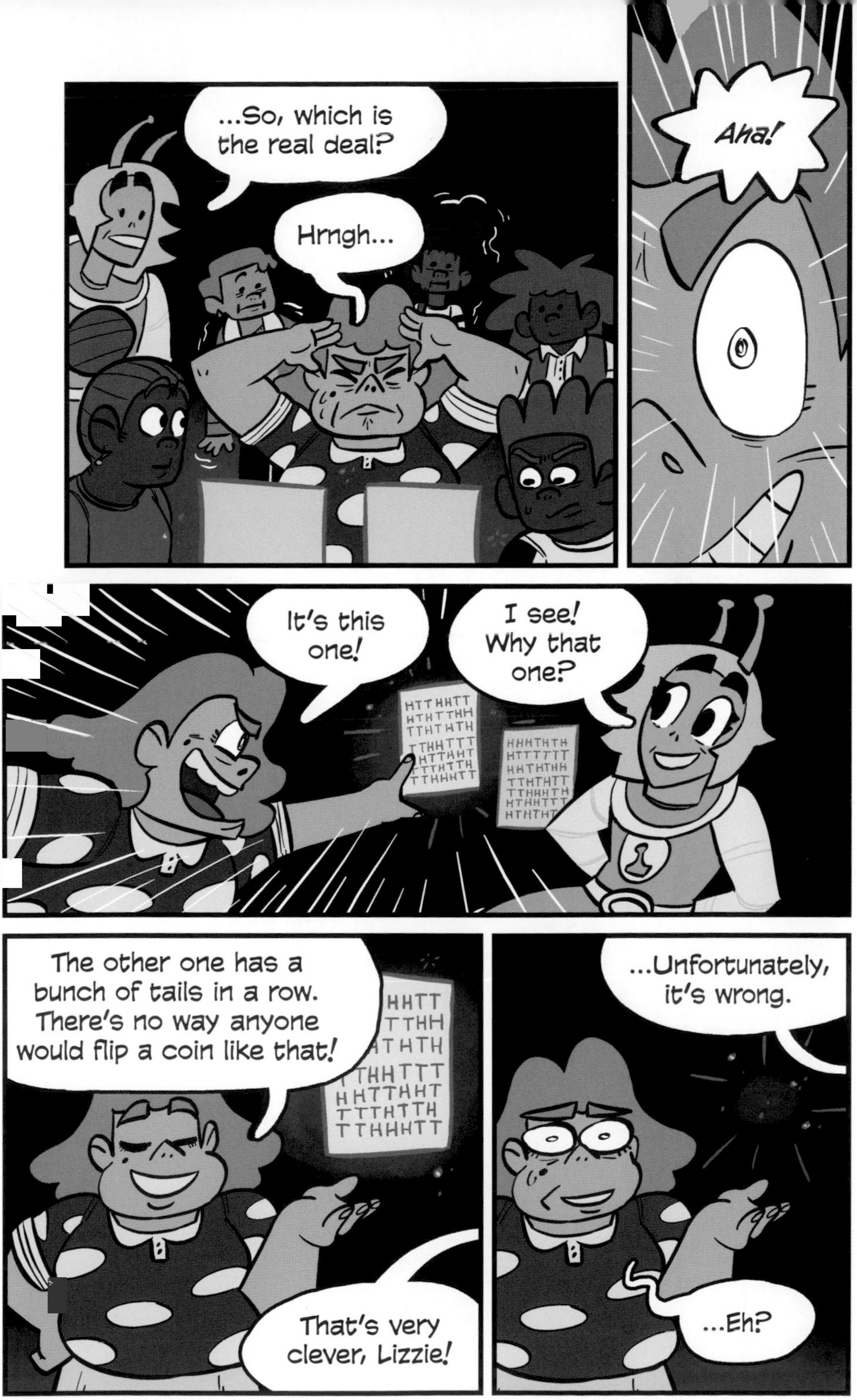
...So, which is the real deal?
Hrngh...
Aha!
It's this one!
I see! Why that one?
The other one has a bunch of tails in a row. There's no way anyone would flip a coin like that!
That's very clever, Lizzie!
...Unfortunately, it's wrong.
...Eh?

44

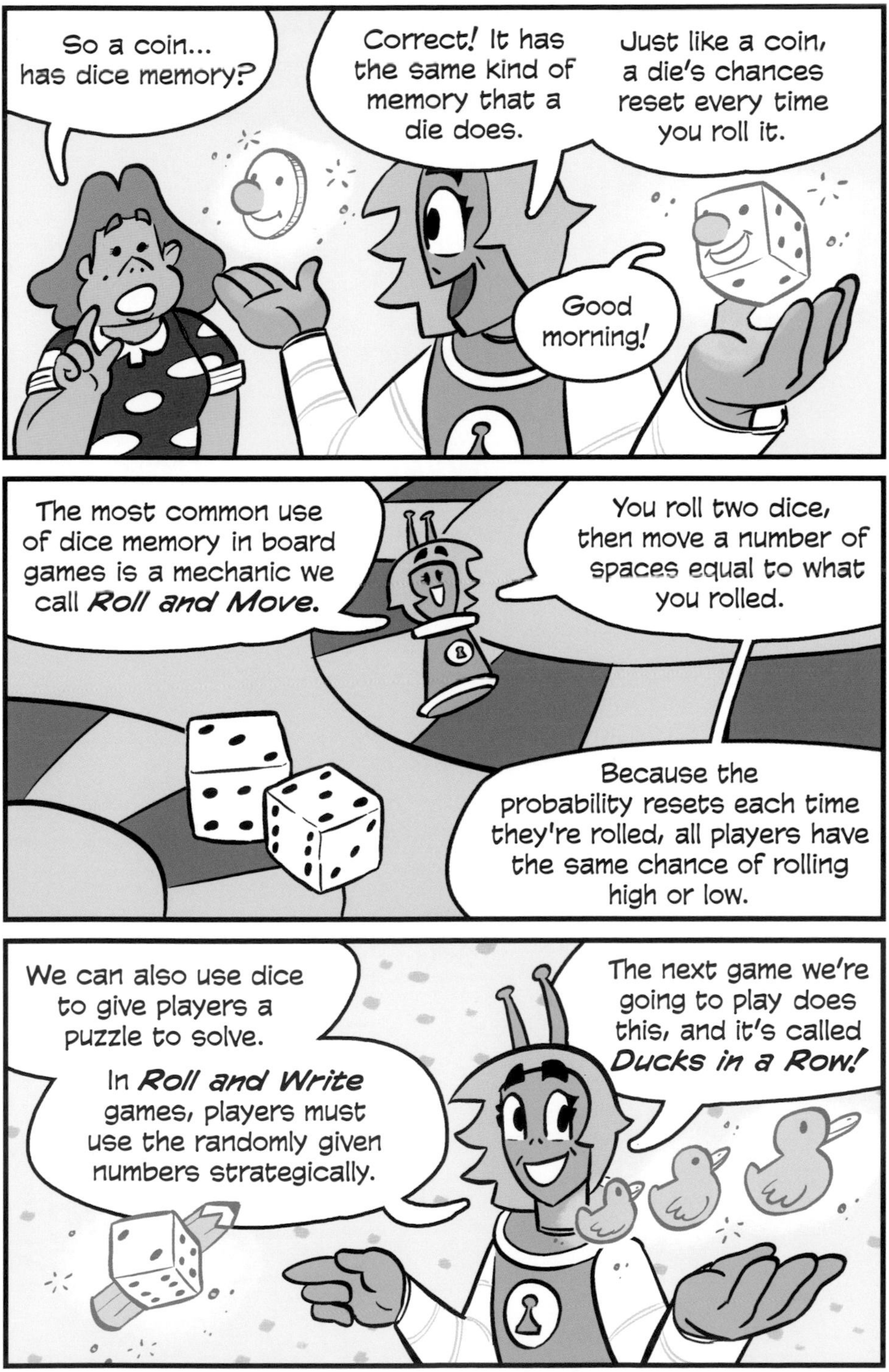
So a coin... has dice memory?
Correct! It has the same kind of memory that a die does.
Just like a coin, a die's chances reset every time you roll it.
Good morning!
The most common use of dice memory in board games is a mechanic we call *Roll and Move.*
You roll two dice, then move a number of spaces equal to what you rolled.
Because the probability resets each time they're rolled, all players have the same chance of rolling high or low.
We can also use dice to give players a puzzle to solve.
In *Roll and Write* games, players must use the randomly given numbers strategically.
The next game we're going to play does this, and it's called *Ducks in a Row!*

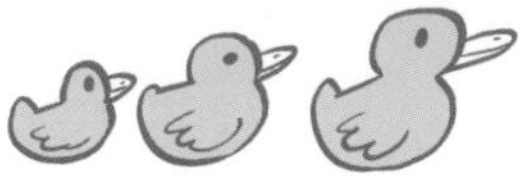

Ducks in a Row

Players:	**Materials:**	**Time to play:**
1+	2 x 6-sided dice, paper, pencil	15+ minutes

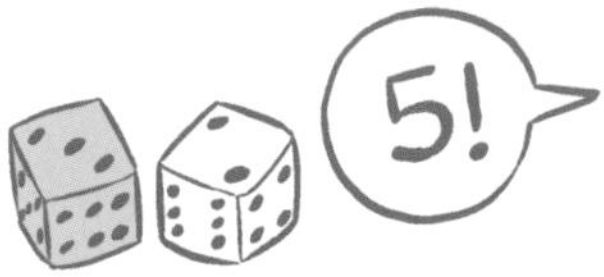
5!

1. Each player draws a row of thirteen boxes or dashes on a sheet of paper.
2. Each turn, one player will roll two dice and call out the sum. All players write this number in one of the boxes on their row. Players can write the called number in any box, as long as it's bigger than (or equal to) every number already written to its left, and smaller than (or equal to) every number already written to its right. Once a box is filled, it cannot be erased.

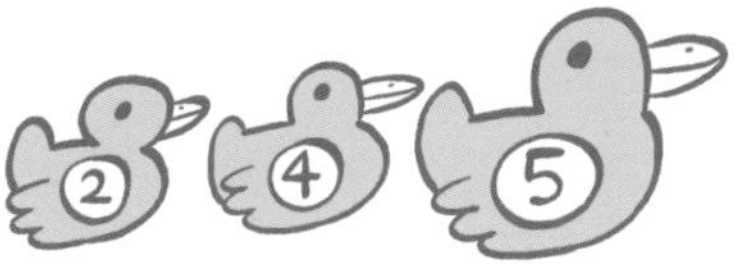
2
4
5

3. If a player can't legally write a called number, they mark a strike above their row. If a player gets three strikes, they're out of the game!

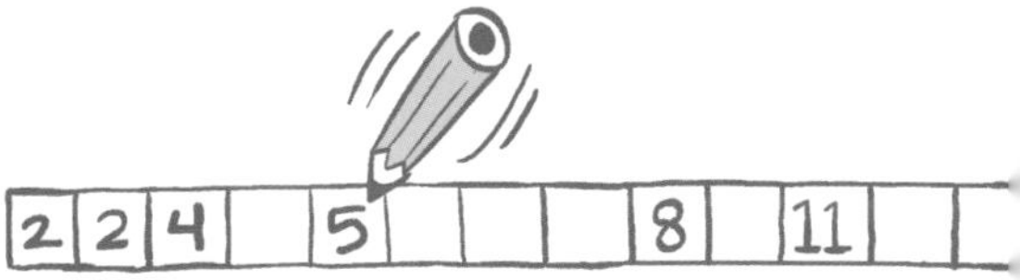
2 2 4 5 8 11

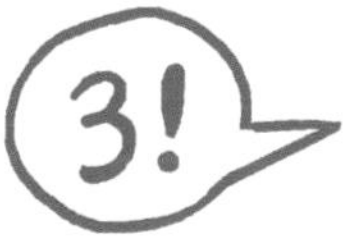
3!

4. The winner is the first player to completely fill their row, or the last player eliminated. (Either way can result in a tie.) In a solo game, you can only win by completely filling your row. If you can't legally place a number, that's a strike. Three strikes and you're out.

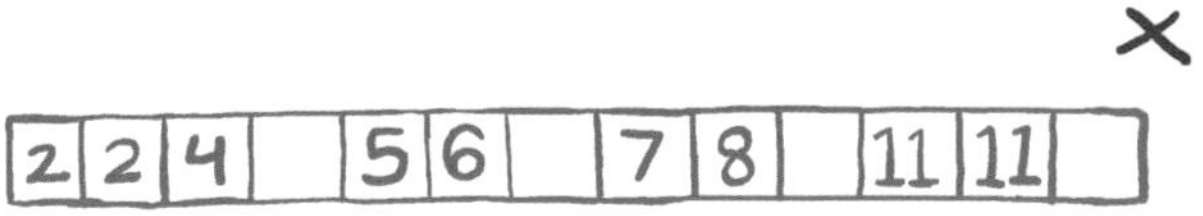
2 2 4 5 6 7 8 11 11

BONUS!

Try playing with different types of dice, and/or more dice per roll. For some truly wild results, use the product of the dice instead of the sum!

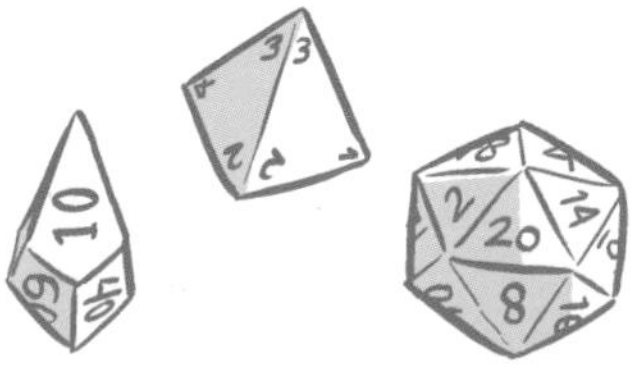

Six-Card Mini Golf

Players: 2	**Materials:** deck of playing cards, pencil, paper	Time to play: 20+ minutes

1. Use a sheet of paper to record the scores. Choose one player to be the dealer. Remove diamonds, spades, and jokers from the deck—they won't be used. Shuffle the deck and deal each player six cards facedown. Do not look at these!

Deck and discard pile

2. Place the deck in the center. Turn its top card faceup and place it next to the deck to start the discard pile.

3. Players arrange their cards in two rows of three, then flip any two of their cards faceup. This area will be called the player's turf. Players cannot look at any facedown cards, even their own.

Turf example

4. Players want to have the *lowest* scoring turf by the end of the round (also called the "hole"). See the scoring guide on the next page for more information.

5. Beginning with the non-dealer, take turns. On your turn, draw the top card from the deck or discard pile. Either discard the drawn card or replace any card in your turf with it, discarding the replaced card. Cards are always drawn, played, and discarded face-up.

Cont. on next page

6. If there are no cards left in the deck at the start of your turn, shuffle the discard pile and create a new deck.

7. The hole immediately ends when a player's turf is completely faceup. Flip the other turf faceup. Calculate each player's scores and write them on the scoresheet. Reshuffle all of the cards and begin a new hole.

Scoring Guide

Ace	1 pt each
2	-2 pts each
3–10	= face value
Jack/Queen	10 pts each
King	0 pts each

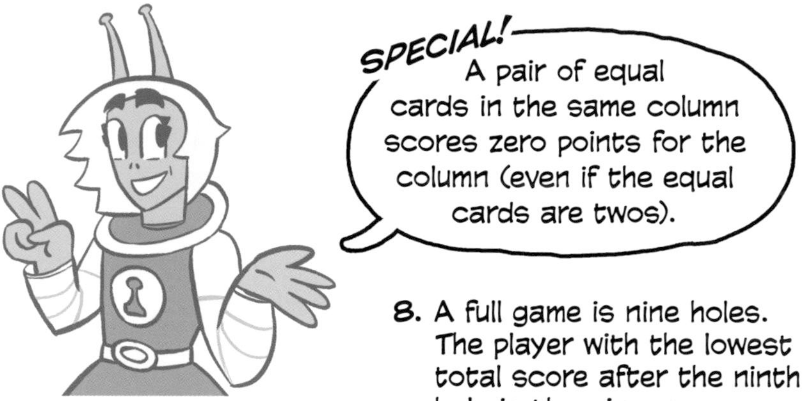
SPECIAL!
A pair of equal cards in the same column scores zero points for the column (even if the equal cards are twos).

8. A full game is nine holes. The player with the lowest total score after the ninth hole is the winner.

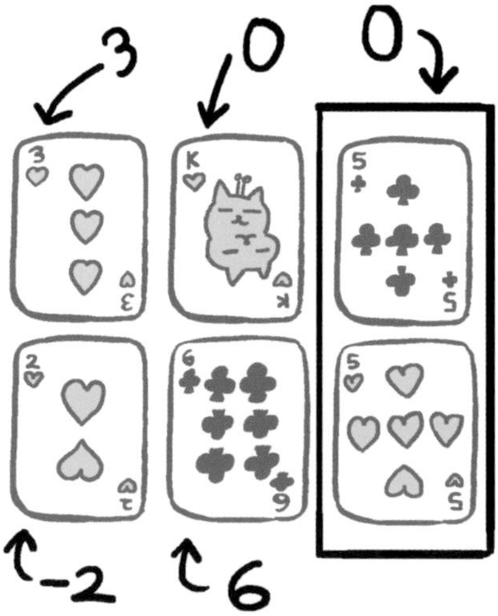
3
0
0
-2
6

Scoring Example

In this example, the player earned a total of 7 points.

Because the two fives are in a column together, they score 0 points instead of 10.

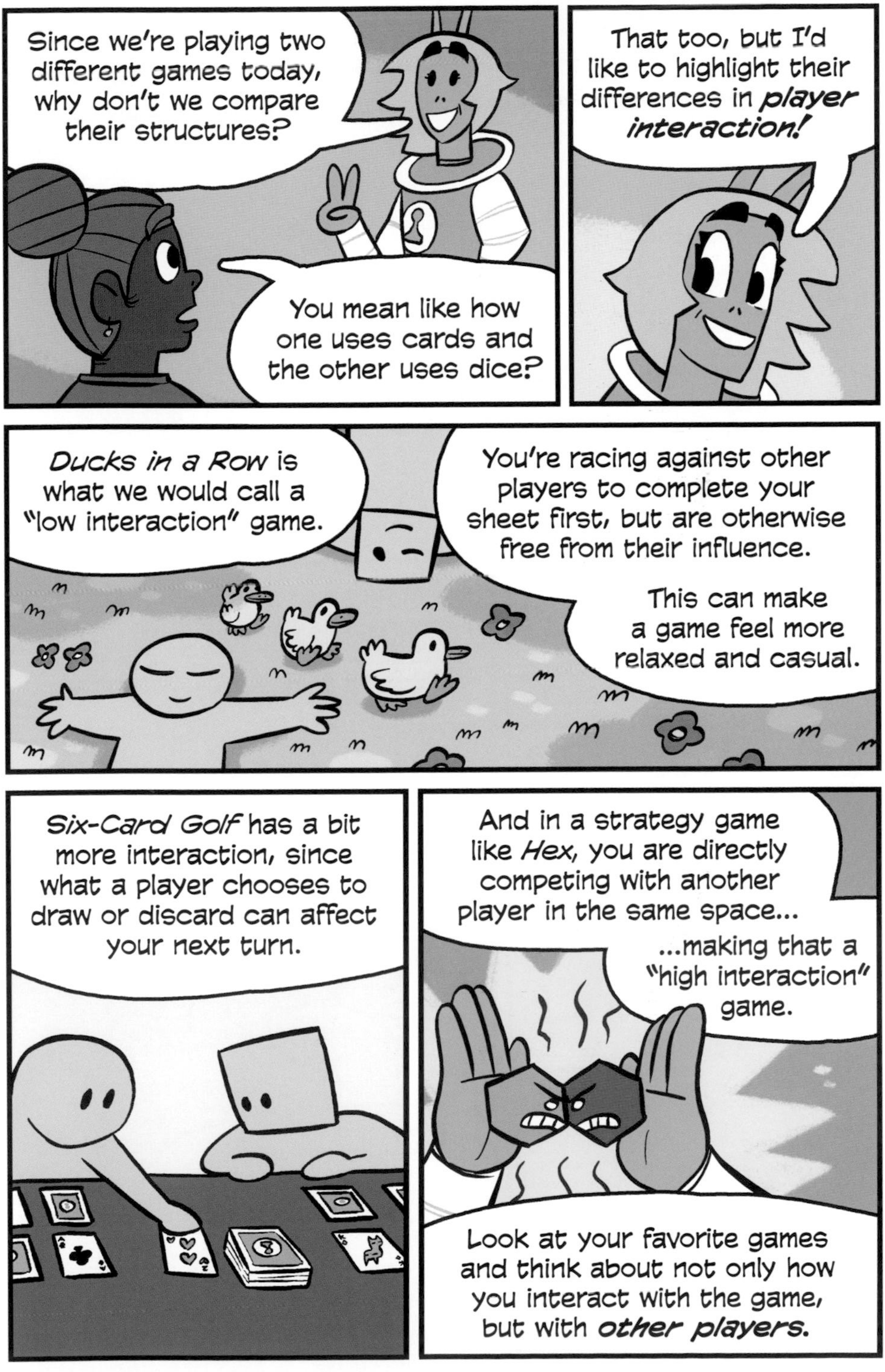

Since we're playing two different games today, why don't we compare their structures?
You mean like how one uses cards and the other uses dice?
That too, but I'd like to highlight their differences in ***player interaction!***
Ducks in a Row is what we would call a "low interaction" game.
You're racing against other players to complete your sheet first, but are otherwise free from their influence.
This can make a game feel more relaxed and casual.
Six-Card Golf has a bit more interaction, since what a player chooses to draw or discard can affect your next turn.
And in a strategy game like *Hex*, you are directly competing with another player in the same space...
...making that a "high interaction" game.
Look at your favorite games and think about not only how you interact with the game, but with ***other players***.

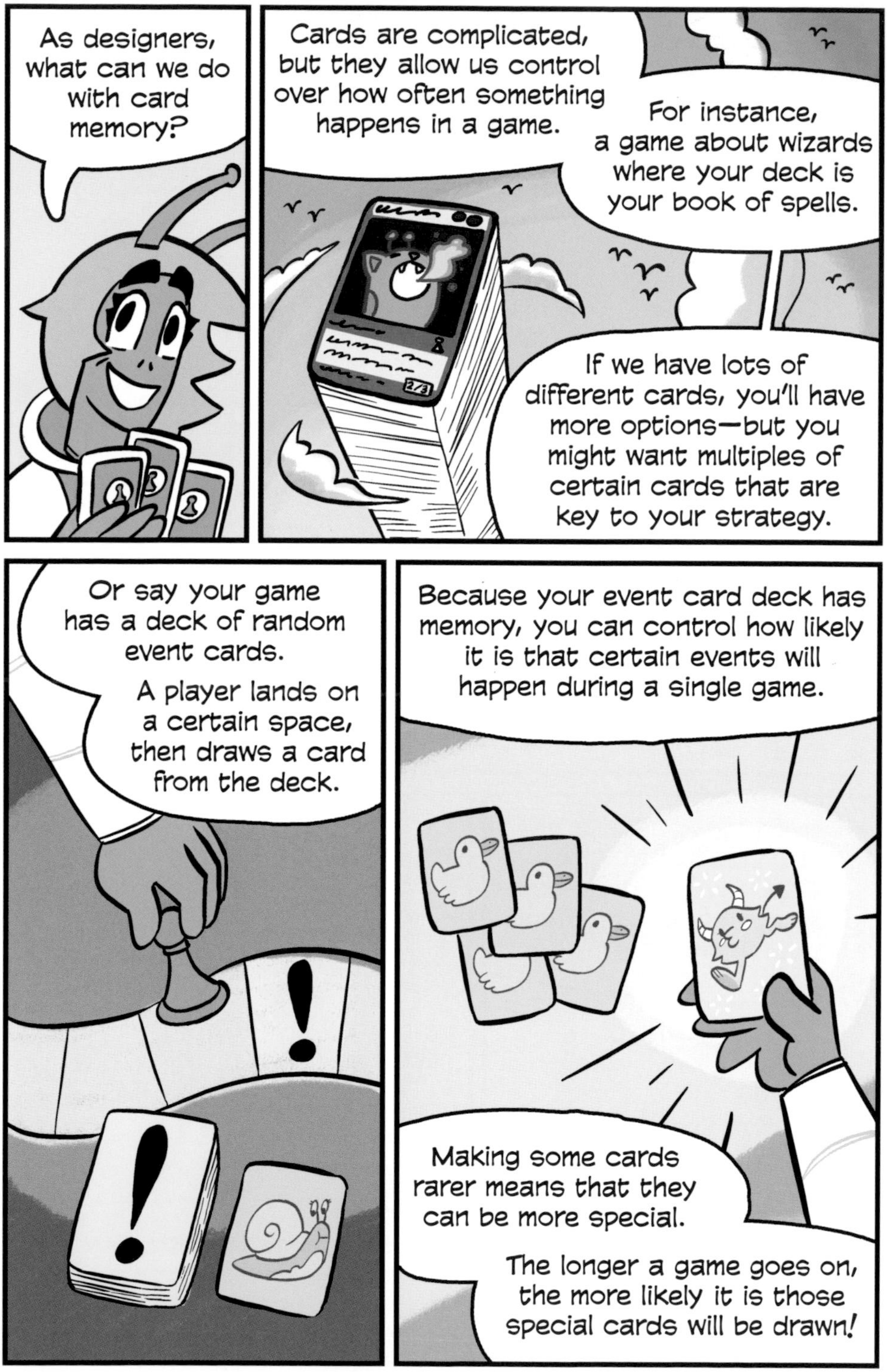

As designers, what can we do with card memory?
Cards are complicated, but they allow us control over how often something happens in a game.
For instance, a game about wizards where your deck is your book of spells.
If we have lots of different cards, you'll have more options—but you might want multiples of certain cards that are key to your strategy.
Or say your game has a deck of random event cards.
A player lands on a certain space, then draws a card from the deck.
Because your event card deck has memory, you can control how likely it is that certain events will happen during a single game.
Making some cards rarer means that they can be more special.
The longer a game goes on, the more likely it is those special cards will be drawn!

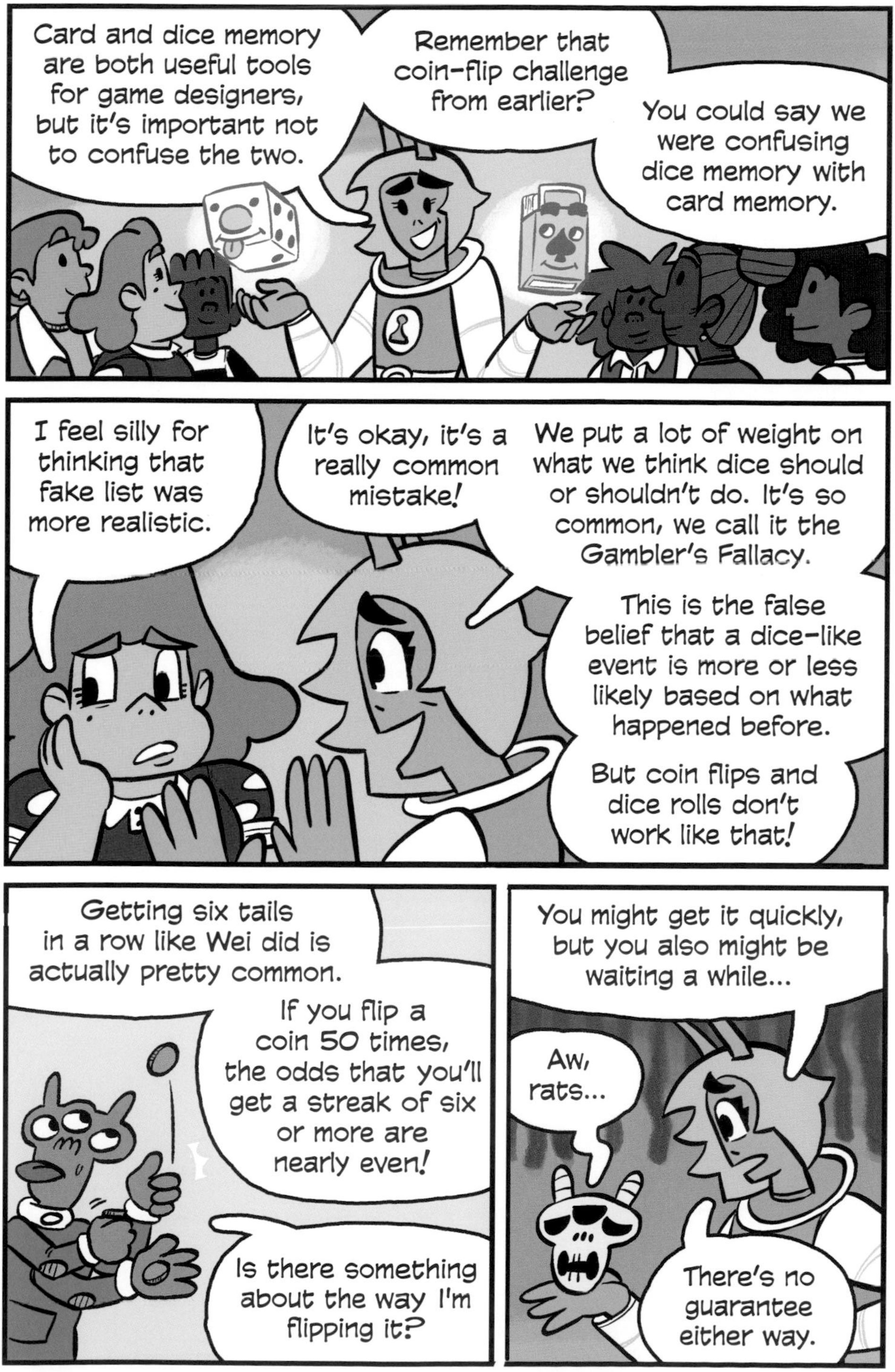
Card and dice memory are both useful tools for game designers, but it's important not to confuse the two.
Remember that coin-flip challenge from earlier?
You could say we were confusing dice memory with card memory.
I feel silly for thinking that fake list was more realistic.
It's okay, it's a really common mistake!
We put a lot of weight on what we think dice should or shouldn't do. It's so common, we call it the Gambler's Fallacy.
This is the false belief that a dice-like event is more or less likely based on what happened before.
But coin flips and dice rolls don't work like that!
Getting six tails in a row like Wei did is actually pretty common.
If you flip a coin 50 times, the odds that you'll get a streak of six or more are nearly even!
Is there something about the way I'm flipping it?
You might get it quickly, but you also might be waiting a while...
Aw, rats...
There's no guarantee either way.

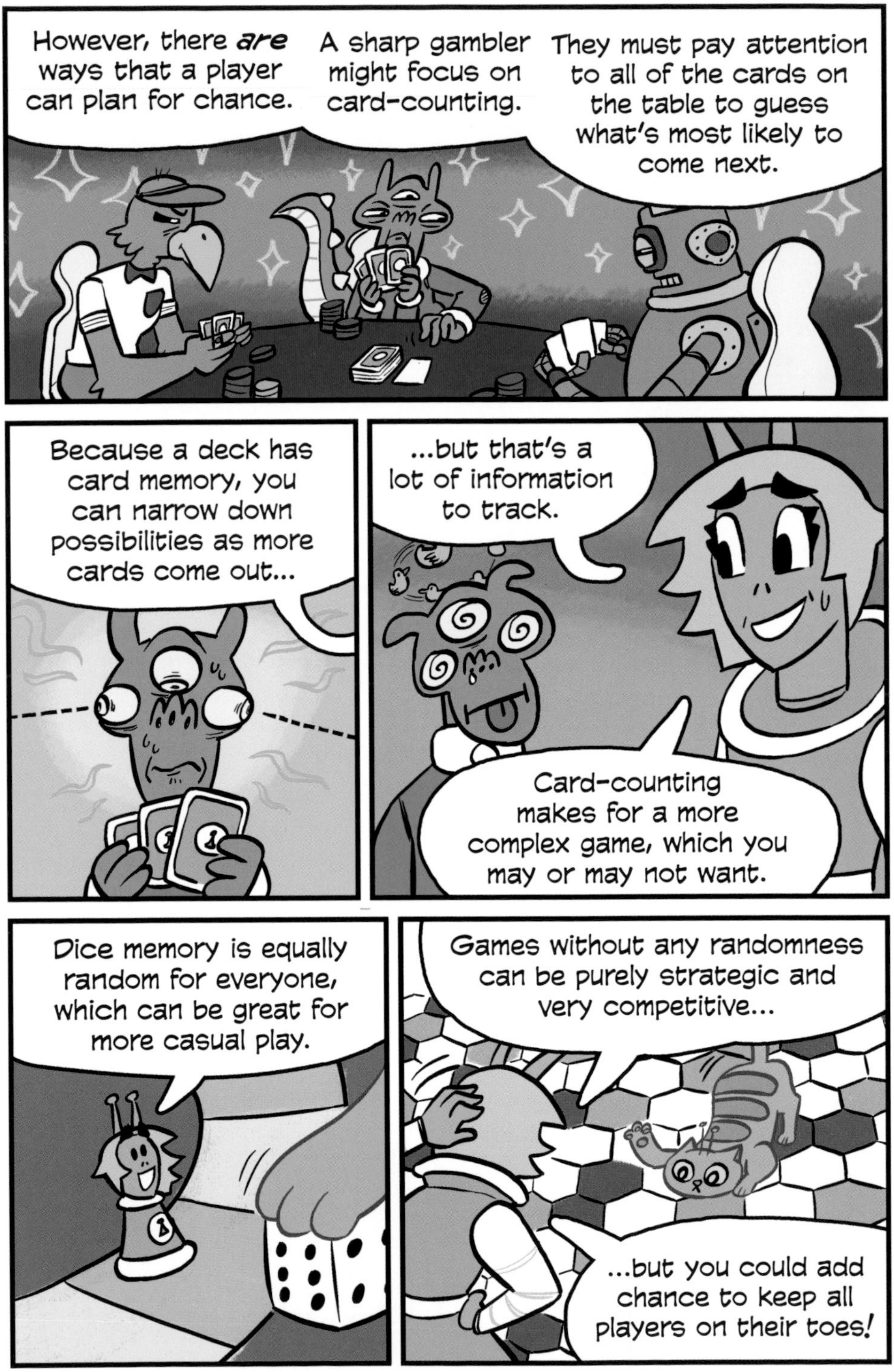
However, there *are* ways that a player can plan for chance.
A sharp gambler might focus on card-counting.
They must pay attention to all of the cards on the table to guess what's most likely to come next.
Because a deck has card memory, you can narrow down possibilities as more cards come out...
...but that's a lot of information to track.
Card-counting makes for a more complex game, which you may or may not want.
Dice memory is equally random for everyone, which can be great for more casual play.
Games without any randomness can be purely strategic and very competitive...
...but you could add chance to keep all players on their toes!

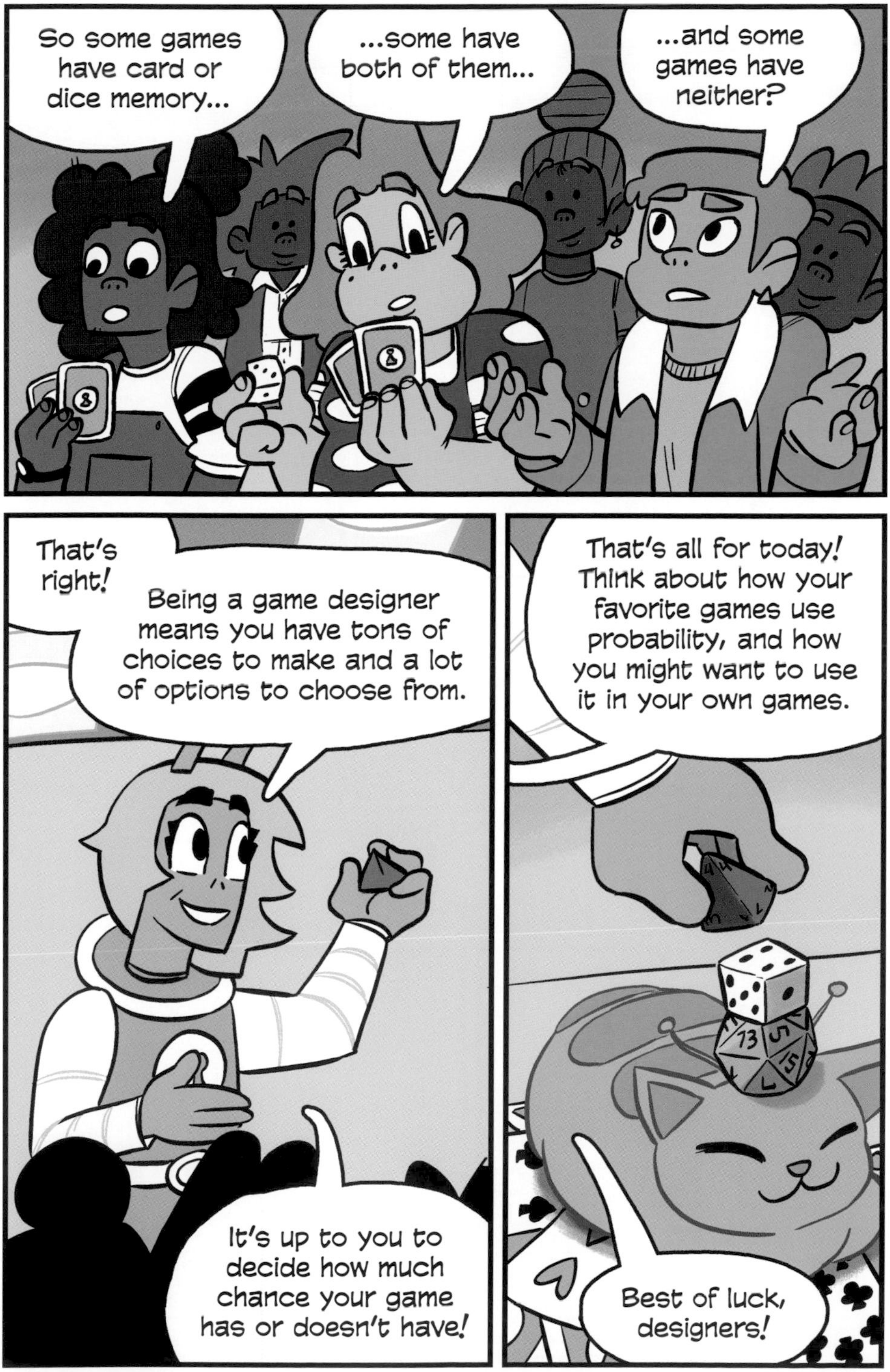
So some games have card or dice memory...
...some have both of them...
...and some games have neither?
That's right!
Being a game designer means you have tons of choices to make and a lot of options to choose from.
It's up to you to decide how much chance your game has or doesn't have!
That's all for today! Think about how your favorite games use probability, and how you might want to use it in your own games.
Best of luck, designers!

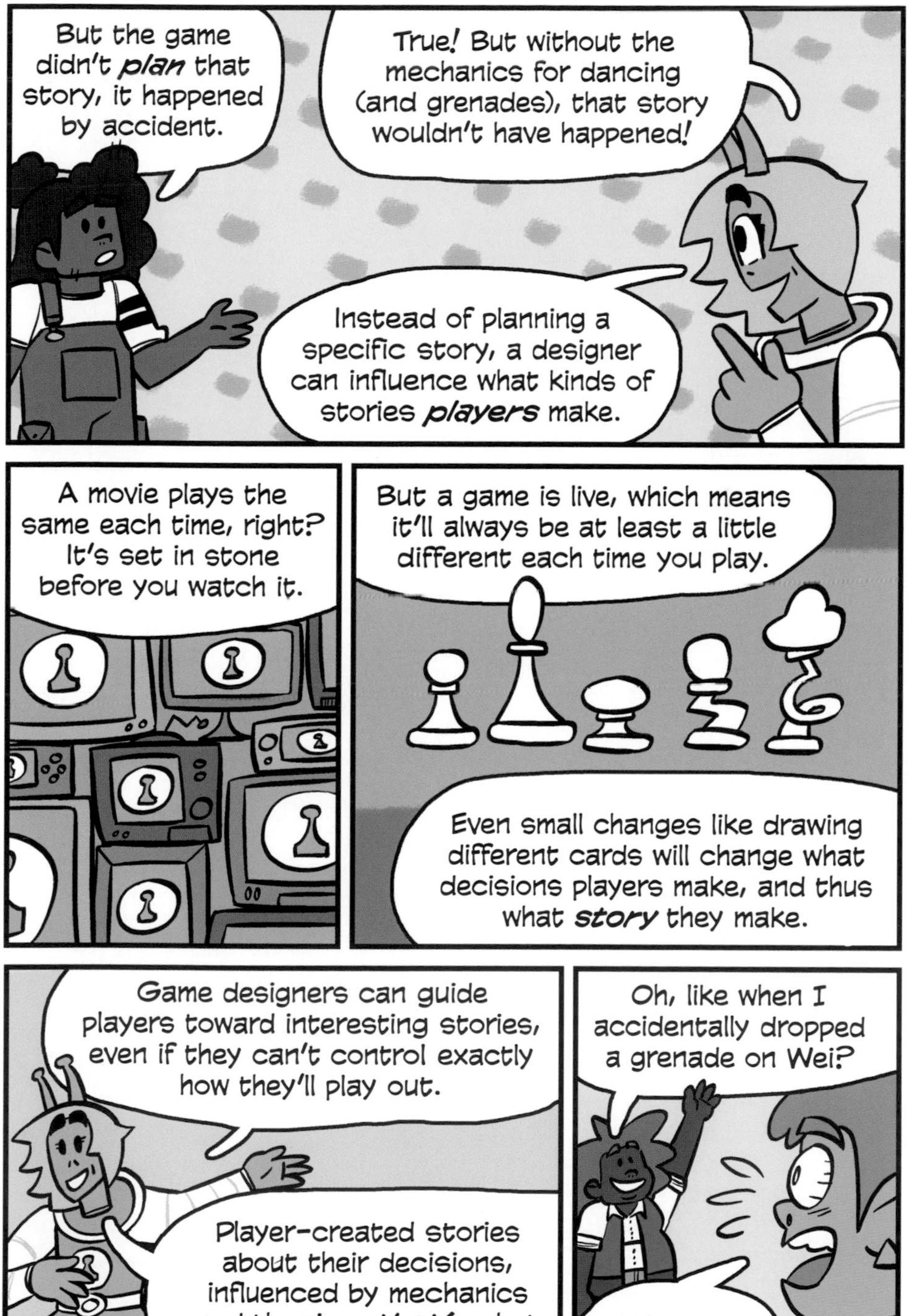
But the game didn't *plan* that story, it happened by accident.
True! But without the mechanics for dancing (and grenades), that story wouldn't have happened!
Instead of planning a specific story, a designer can influence what kinds of stories *players* make.
A movie plays the same each time, right? It's set in stone before you watch it.
But a game is live, which means it'll always be at least a little different each time you play.
Even small changes like drawing different cards will change what decisions players make, and thus what *story* they make.
Game designers can guide players toward interesting stories, even if they can't control exactly how they'll play out.
Player-created stories about their decisions, influenced by mechanics and theming: *that's* what we're talking about today.
Oh, like when I accidentally dropped a grenade on Wei?
THAT WAS YOU?!

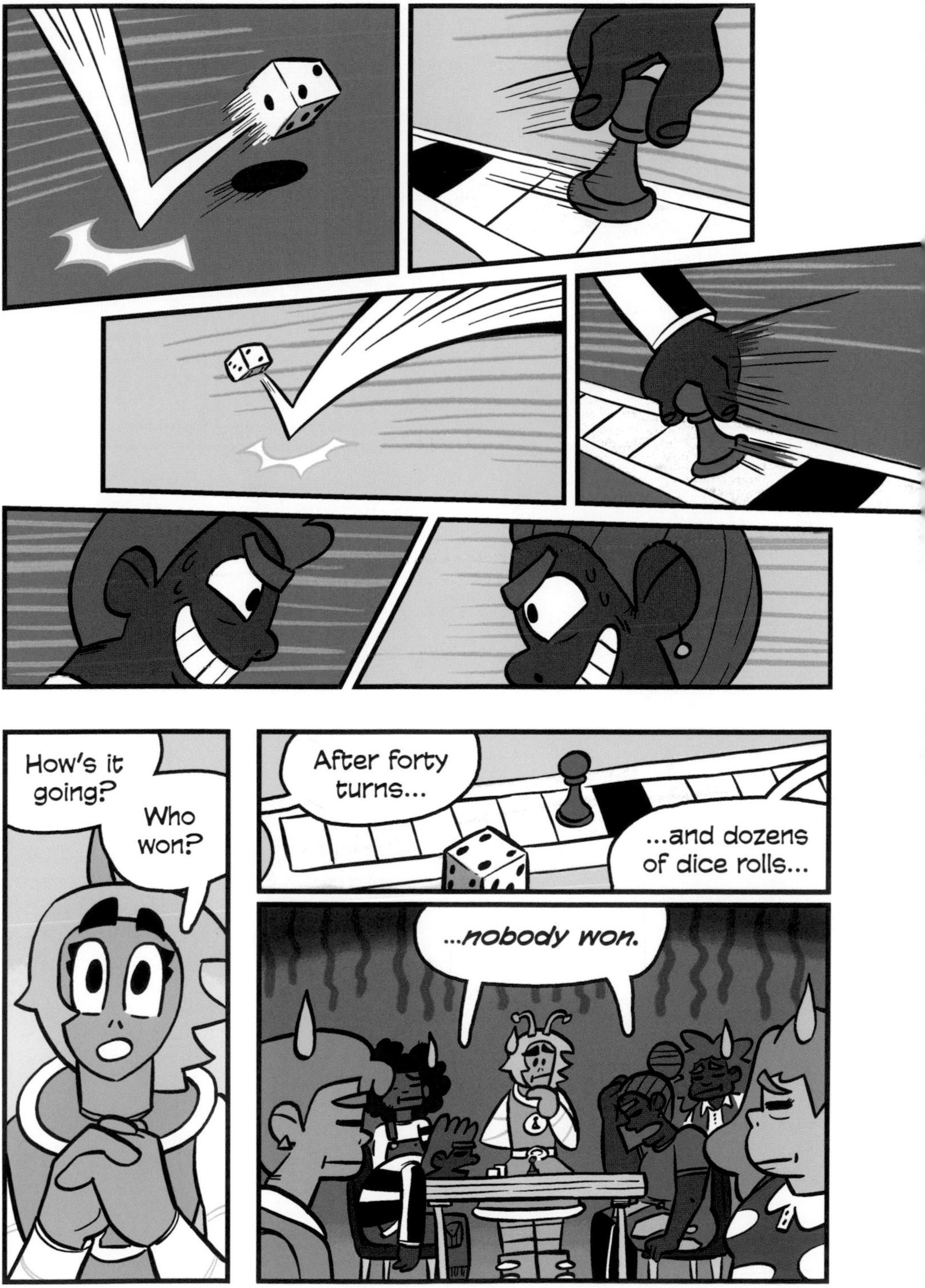
How's it going?
Who won?
After forty turns...
...and dozens of dice rolls...
...nobody won.

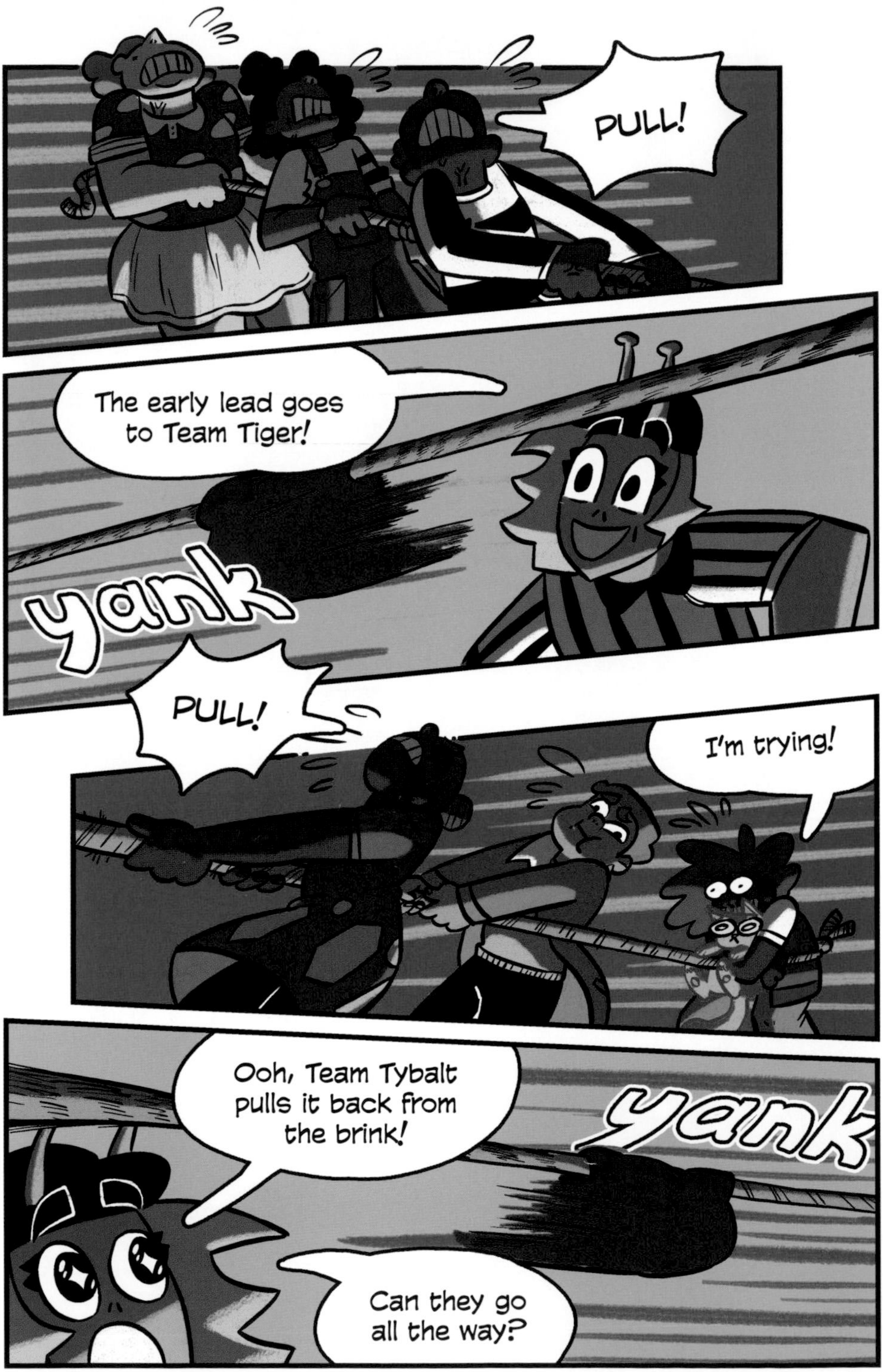
PULL!
The early lead goes to Team Tiger!
yank
PULL!
I'm trying!
Ooh, Team Tybalt pulls it back from the brink!
yank
Can they go all the way?

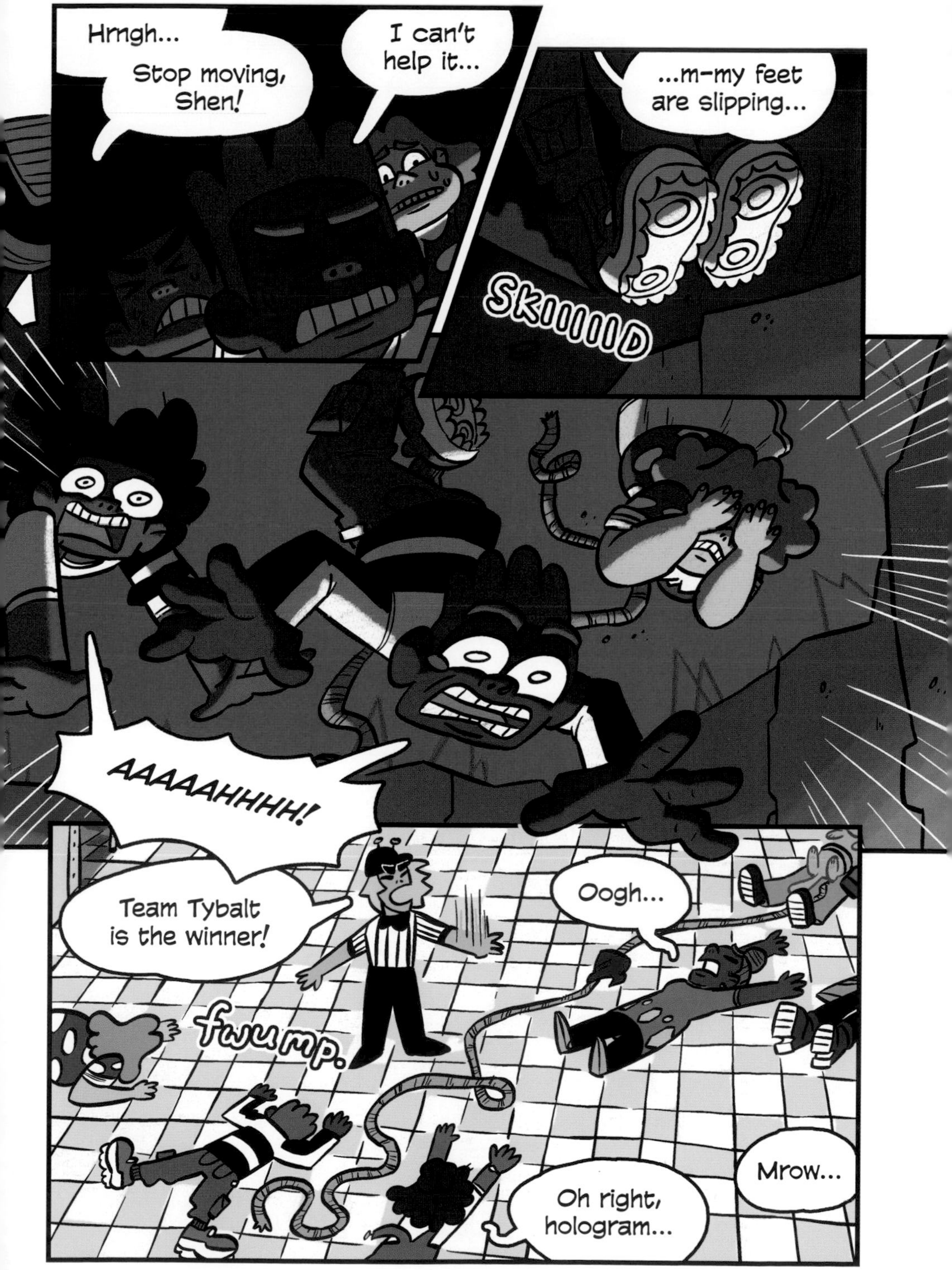
Hrngh...
Stop moving, Shen!
I can't help it...
...m-my feet are slipping...
SKIIIIID
AAAAAHHHH!
Team Tybalt is the winner!
Oogh...
fwump.
Mrow...
Oh right, hologram...

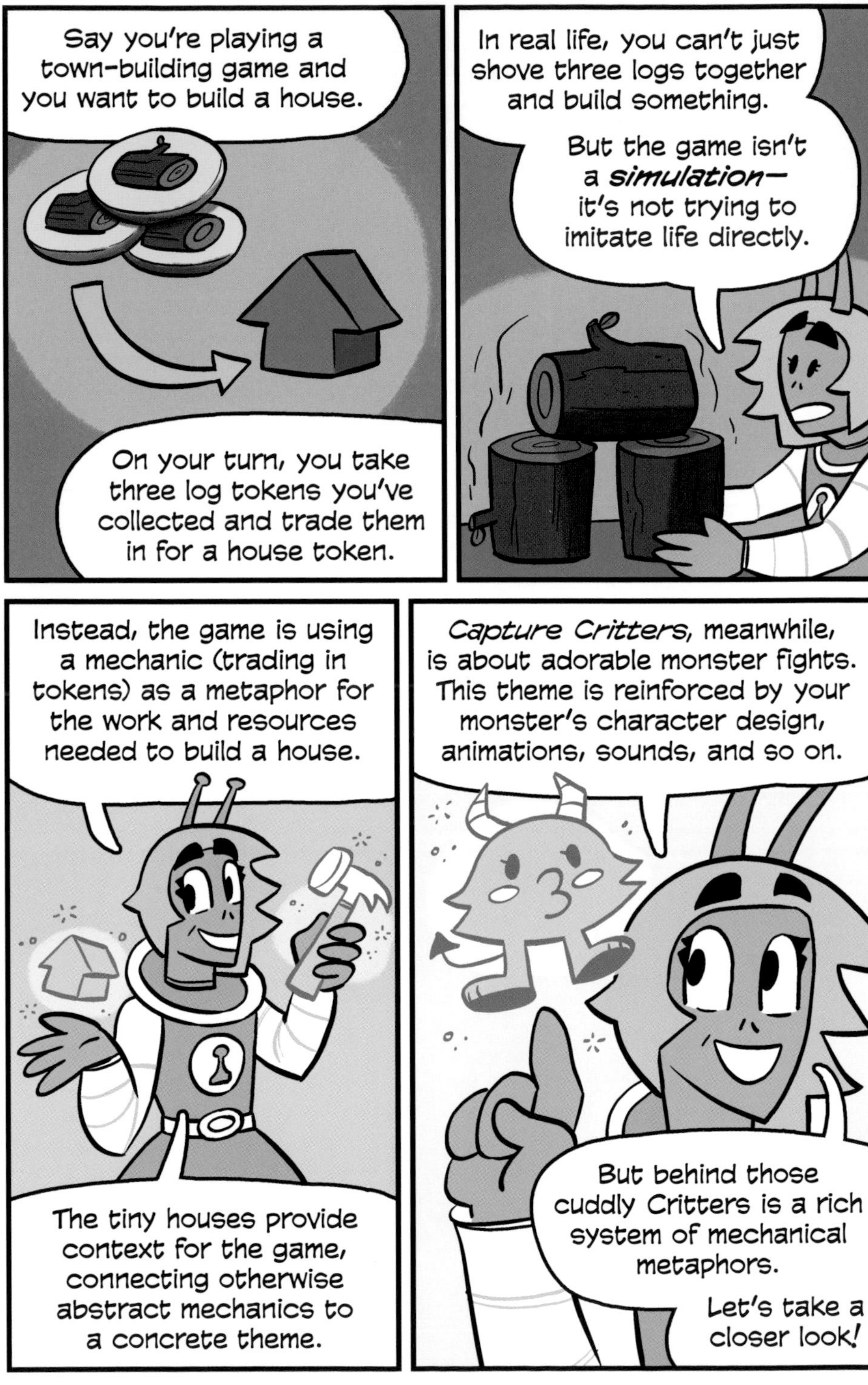
Say you're playing a town-building game and you want to build a house.
On your turn, you take three log tokens you've collected and trade them in for a house token.
In real life, you can't just shove three logs together and build something.
But the game isn't a ***simulation***—it's not trying to imitate life directly.
Instead, the game is using a mechanic (trading in tokens) as a metaphor for the work and resources needed to build a house.
The tiny houses provide context for the game, connecting otherwise abstract mechanics to a concrete theme.
Capture Critters, meanwhile, is about adorable monster fights. This theme is reinforced by your monster's character design, animations, sounds, and so on.
But behind those cuddly Critters is a rich system of mechanical metaphors.
Let's take a closer look!

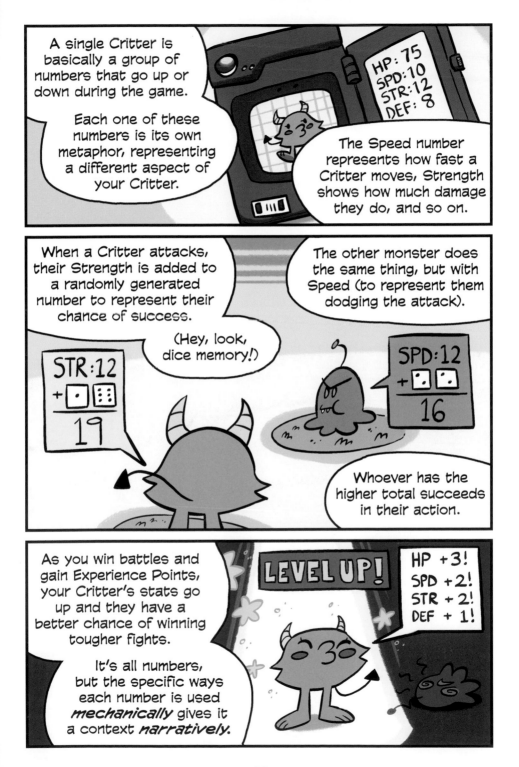

A single Critter is basically a group of numbers that go up or down during the game.

Each one of these numbers is its own metaphor, representing a different aspect of your Critter.

HP: 75
SPD: 10
STR: 12
DEF: 8

The Speed number represents how fast a Critter moves, Strength shows how much damage they do, and so on.

When a Critter attacks, their Strength is added to a randomly generated number to represent their chance of success.

(Hey, look, dice memory!)

STR: 12
+ □ □
19

The other monster does the same thing, but with Speed (to represent them dodging the attack).

SPD: 12
+ □ □
16

Whoever has the higher total succeeds in their action.

As you win battles and gain Experience Points, your Critter's stats go up and they have a better chance of winning tougher fights.

It's all numbers, but the specific ways each number is used *mechanically* gives it a context *narratively*.

LEVEL UP!

HP +3!
SPD +2!
STR +2!
DEF +1!

69

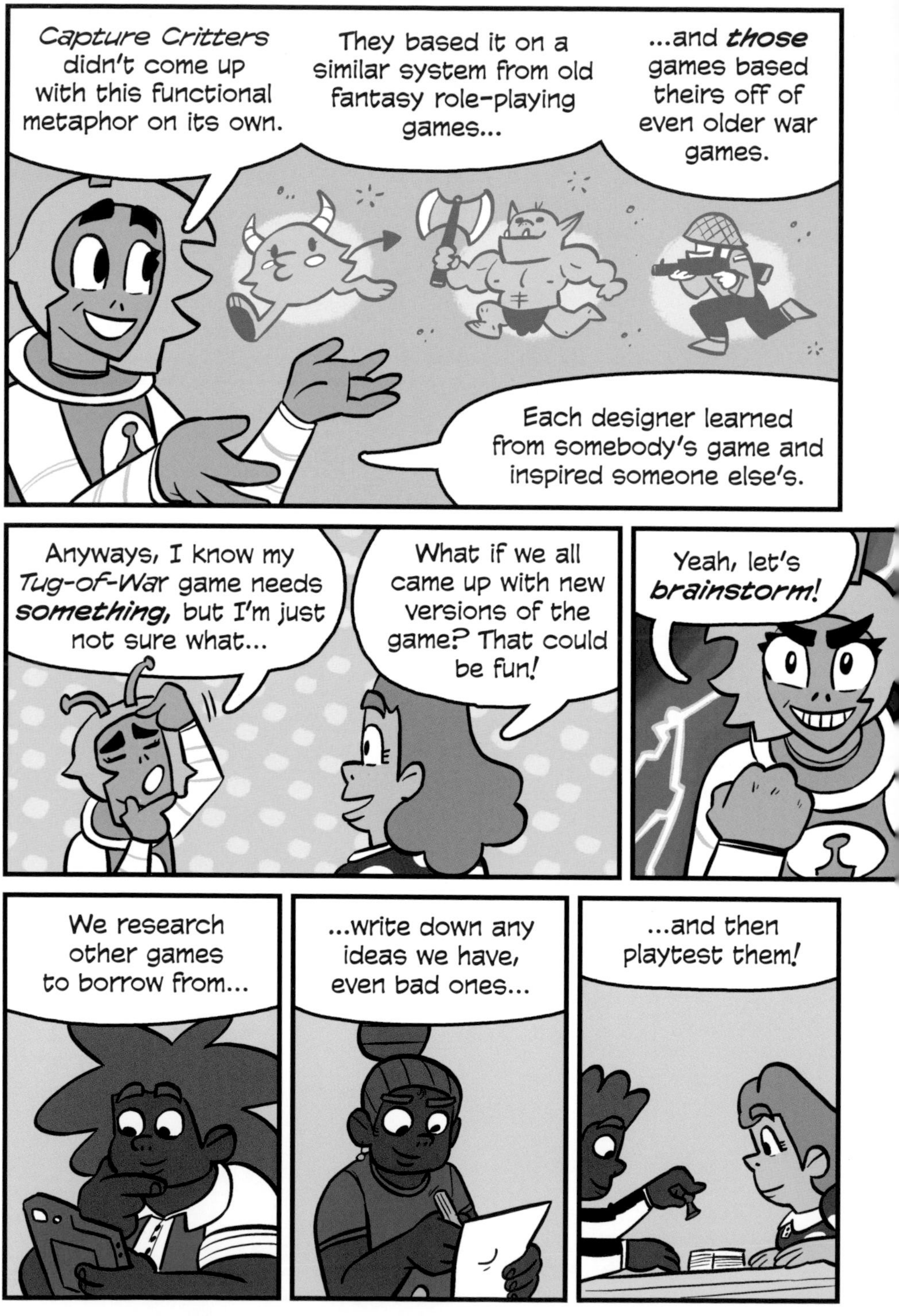
Capture Critters didn't come up with this functional metaphor on its own.
They based it on a similar system from old fantasy role-playing games...
...and ***those*** games based theirs off of even older war games.
Each designer learned from somebody's game and inspired someone else's.
Anyways, I know my *Tug-of-War* game needs ***something***, but I'm just not sure what...
What if we all came up with new versions of the game? That could be fun!
Yeah, let's ***brainstorm***!
We research other games to borrow from...
...write down any ideas we have, even bad ones...
...and then playtest them!

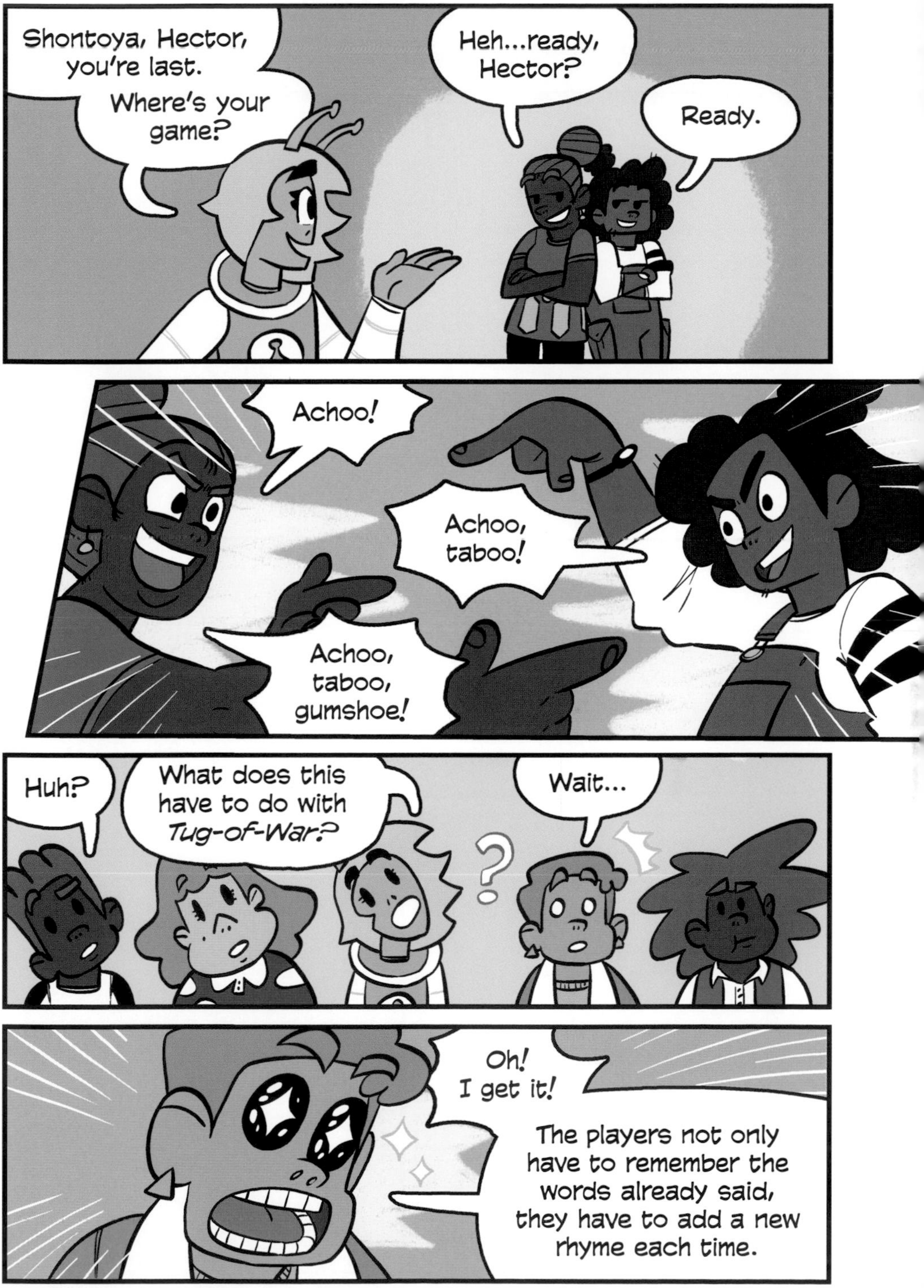
Shontoya, Hector, you're last.
Where's your game?
Heh...ready, Hector?
Ready.
Achoo!
Achoo, taboo!
Achoo, taboo, gumshoe!
Huh?
What does this have to do with *Tug-of-War?*
Wait...
Oh! I get it!
The players not only have to remember the words already said, they have to add a new rhyme each time.

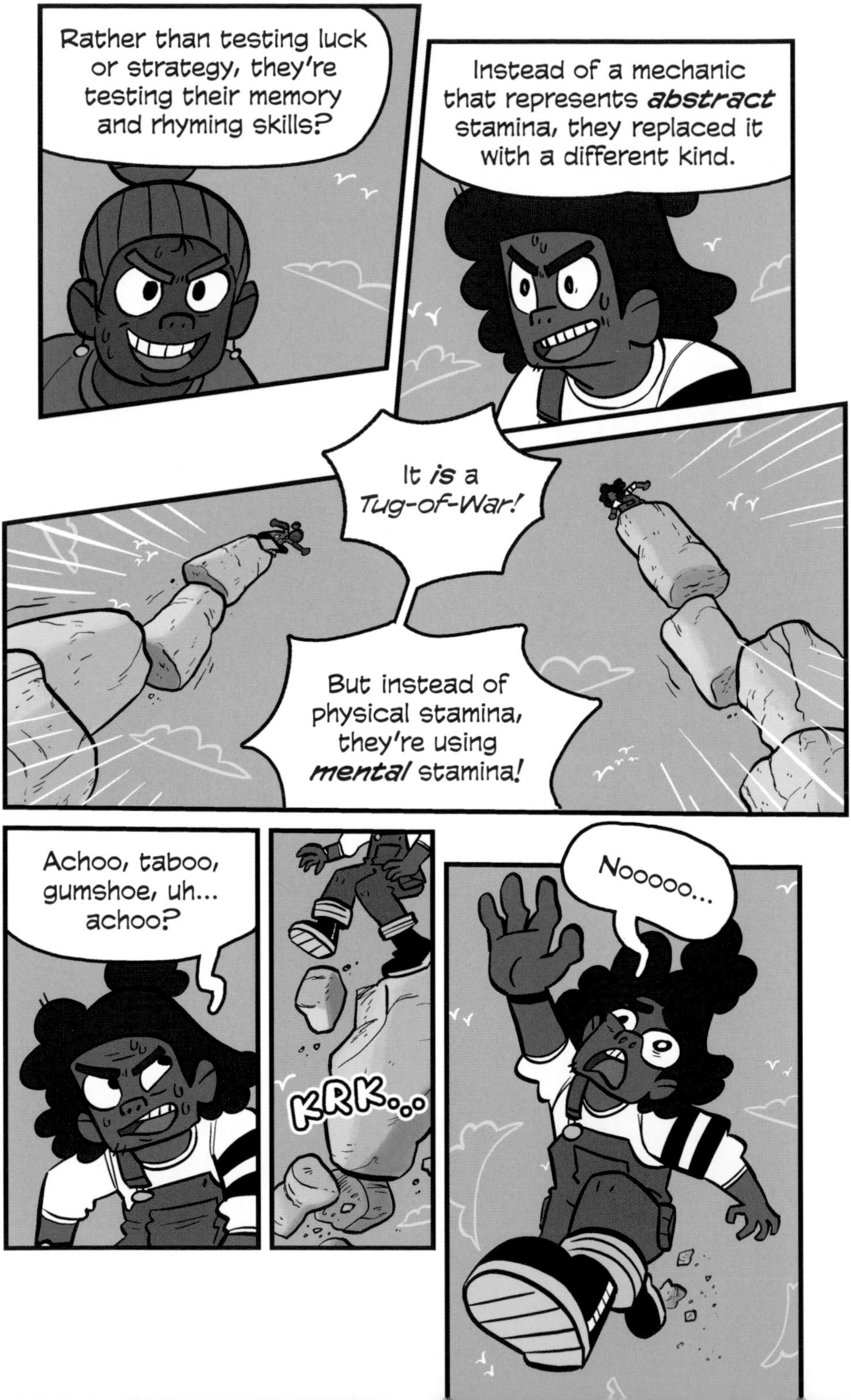

Rather than testing luck or strategy, they're testing their memory and rhyming skills?
Instead of a mechanic that represents *abstract* stamina, they replaced it with a different kind.
It *is* a *Tug-of-War!*
But instead of physical stamina, they're using *mental* stamina!
Achoo, taboo, gumshoe, uh... achoo?
KRK...
Nooooo...

A game's theming doesn't have to directly correlate with its mechanics.

Sometimes, it's just to add flavor.

As we've seen, a game can also be completely abstract and have *no* theming.

The important thing is that playing the game creates a satisfying experience.

We have more to cover, but you've already displayed some brilliant ideas!

For the next couple days, you'll be making your own totally new game to show off at the end of camp!

If you get stuck, make a list of themes and activities you like and a big list of mechanics from games that you enjoy playing.

Mix and match from the lists to see what stands out for you.

I'm excited to see what you all make!

Heh, she called me brilliant.

She wasn't talking about *you*...

Your game designer story is just starting!

Brainstorming and Game Research!

This is a creative exercise to brainstorm ideas for a totally new game project. All you'll need is a couple sheets of paper and a pencil or pen!

Part One: Mind Map

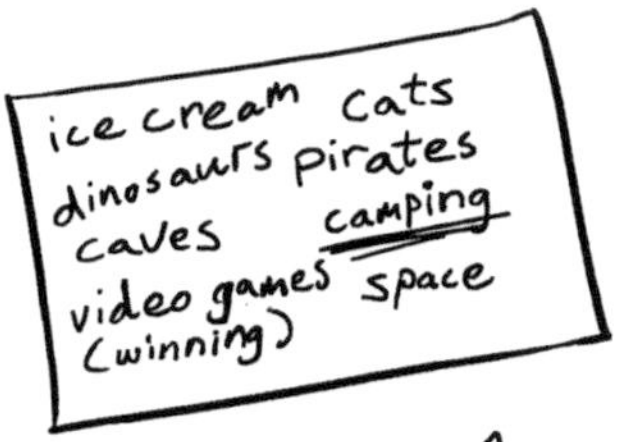

1. Make a list of topics and activities you enjoy. Try to come up with at least ten items!

2. Choose one of these items to be the subject of your mind map. Write it in the center of a new sheet of paper.

3. Draw lines outward from the center, and add aspects related to your item. Use a highlighter or add a star to aspects you are most interested in.

Part Two: Research

1. Look up games with your mind map's theme. Hint: add 'bgg' to the end of your search!* If you have trouble finding any, try looking up the associated subjects or concepts.

2. Choose one of the games and research how it plays. Most games will have their manual or video tutorials freely available online. You may also be able to borrow or try the game at a local game store.

3. Describe the game's mechanics. How do they relate to the game's theming? How do the game's aesthetics support this theme? Does playing this game feel like it embodies the theme?

You may repeat these steps with other items from your list. Use these to begin thinking about how you might design a game to embody your favorite things.

* boardgamegeek.com, or BGG, is an online resource for board game and card game enthusiasts.

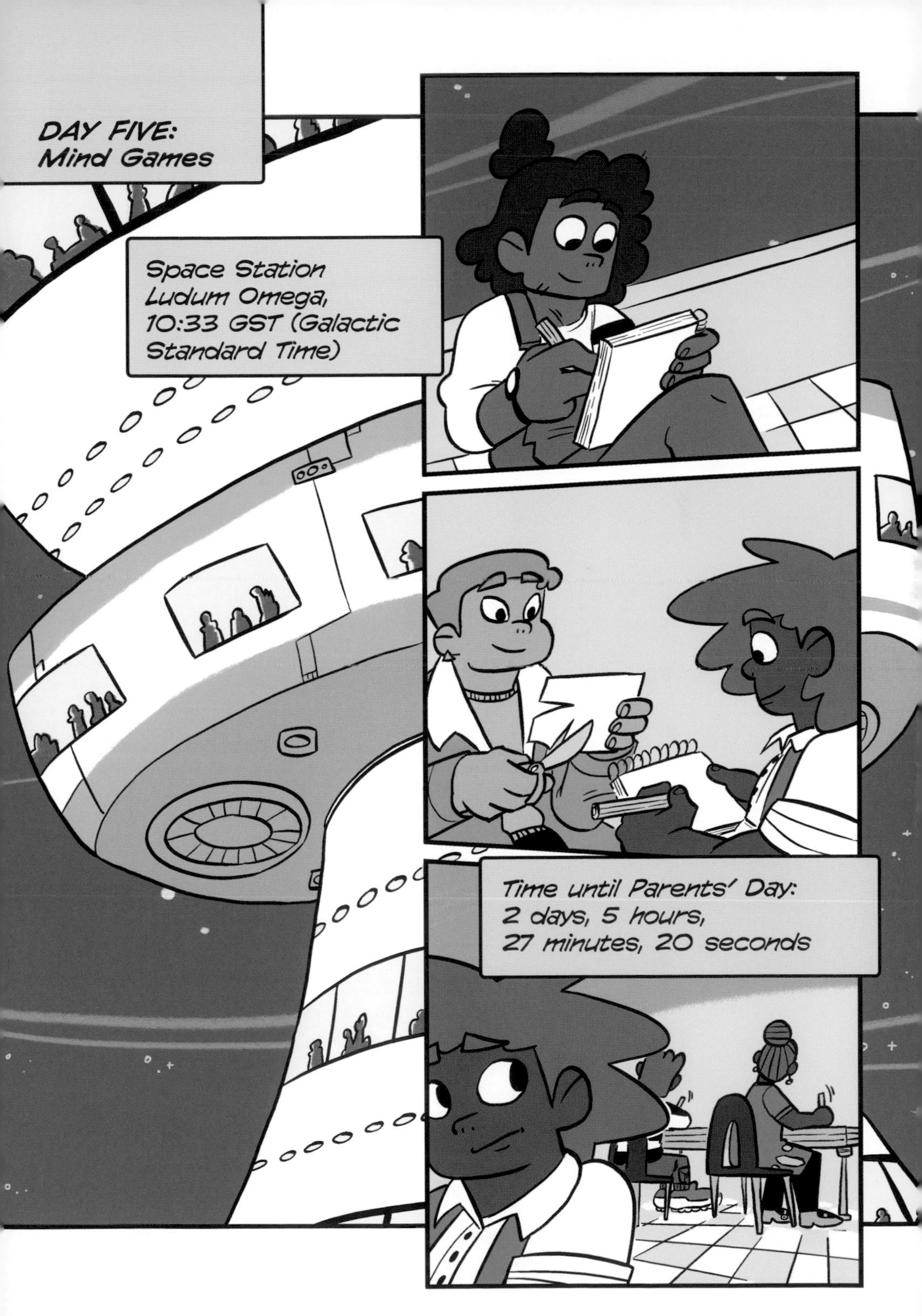
DAY FIVE:
Mind Games
Space Station
Ludum Omega,
10:33 GST (Galactic
Standard Time)
Time until Parents' Day:
2 days, 5 hours,
27 minutes, 20 seconds

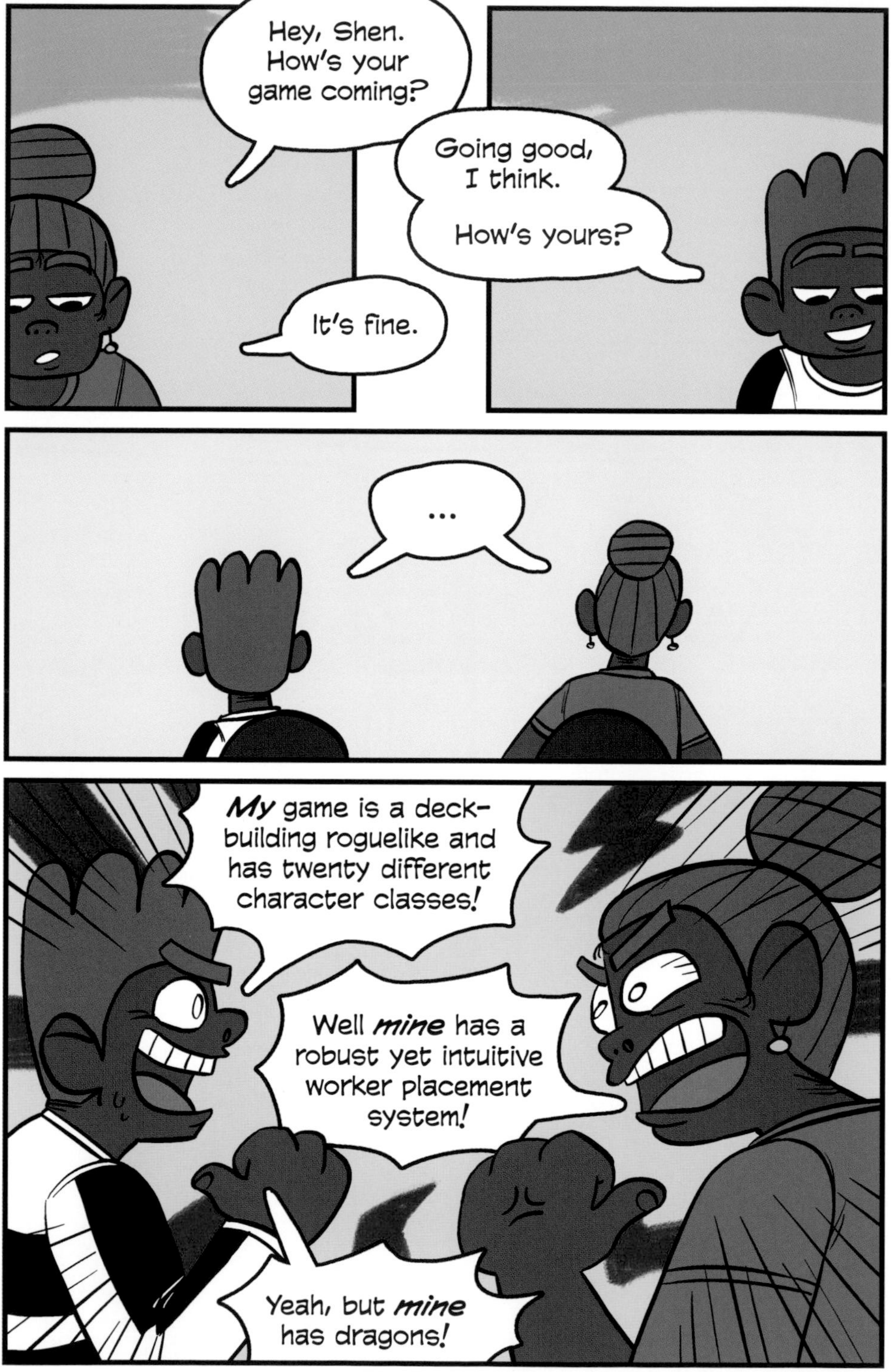
Hey, Shen. How's your game coming?
It's fine.
Going good, I think.
How's yours?
...
My game is a deck-building roguelike and has twenty different character classes!
Well *mine* has a robust yet intuitive worker placement system!
Yeah, but *mine* has dragons!

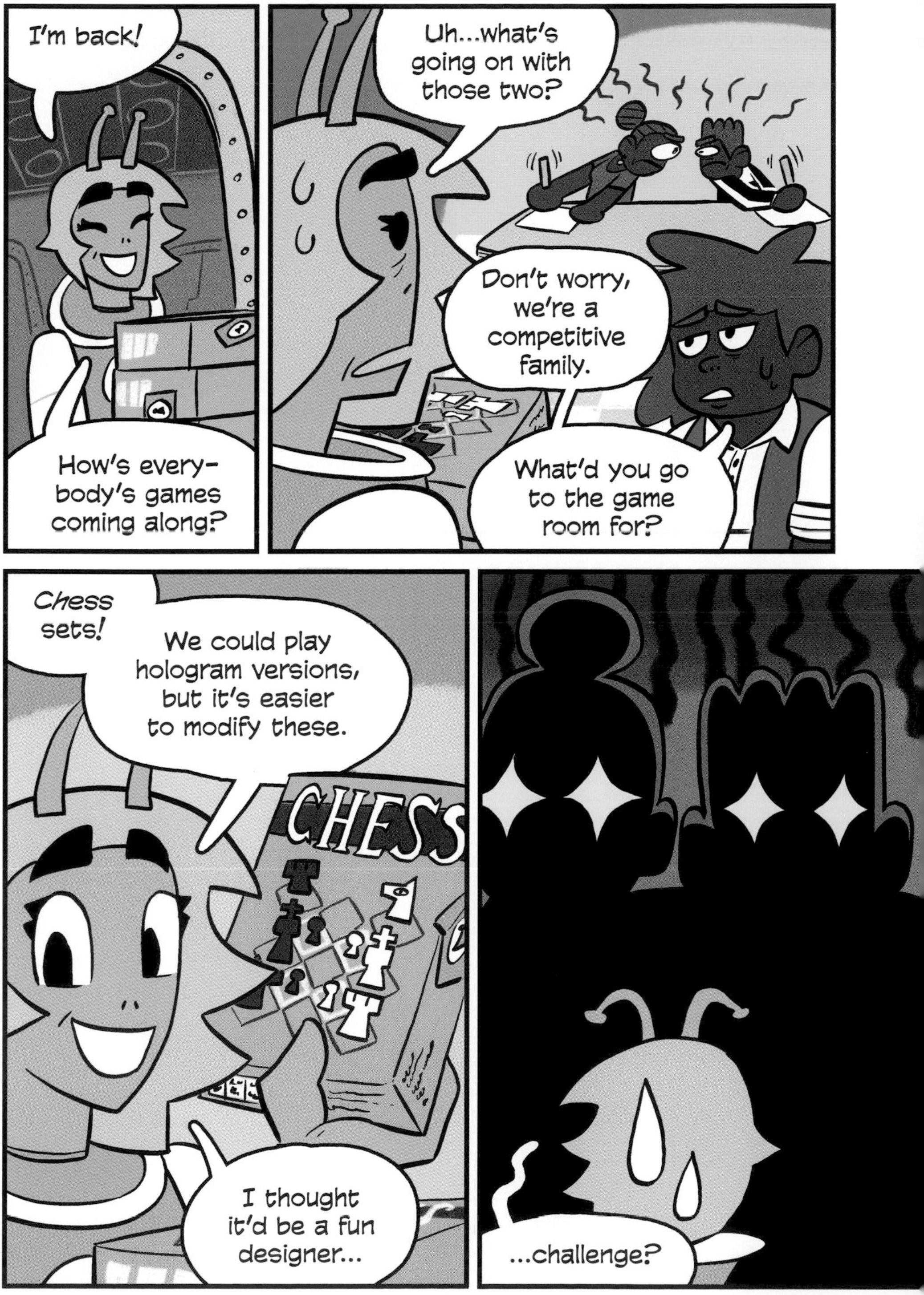
I'm back!
How's every-body's games coming along?
Uh...what's going on with those two?
Don't worry, we're a competitive family.
What'd you go to the game room for?
Chess sets!
We could play hologram versions, but it's easier to modify these.
CHESS
I thought it'd be a fun designer...
...challenge?

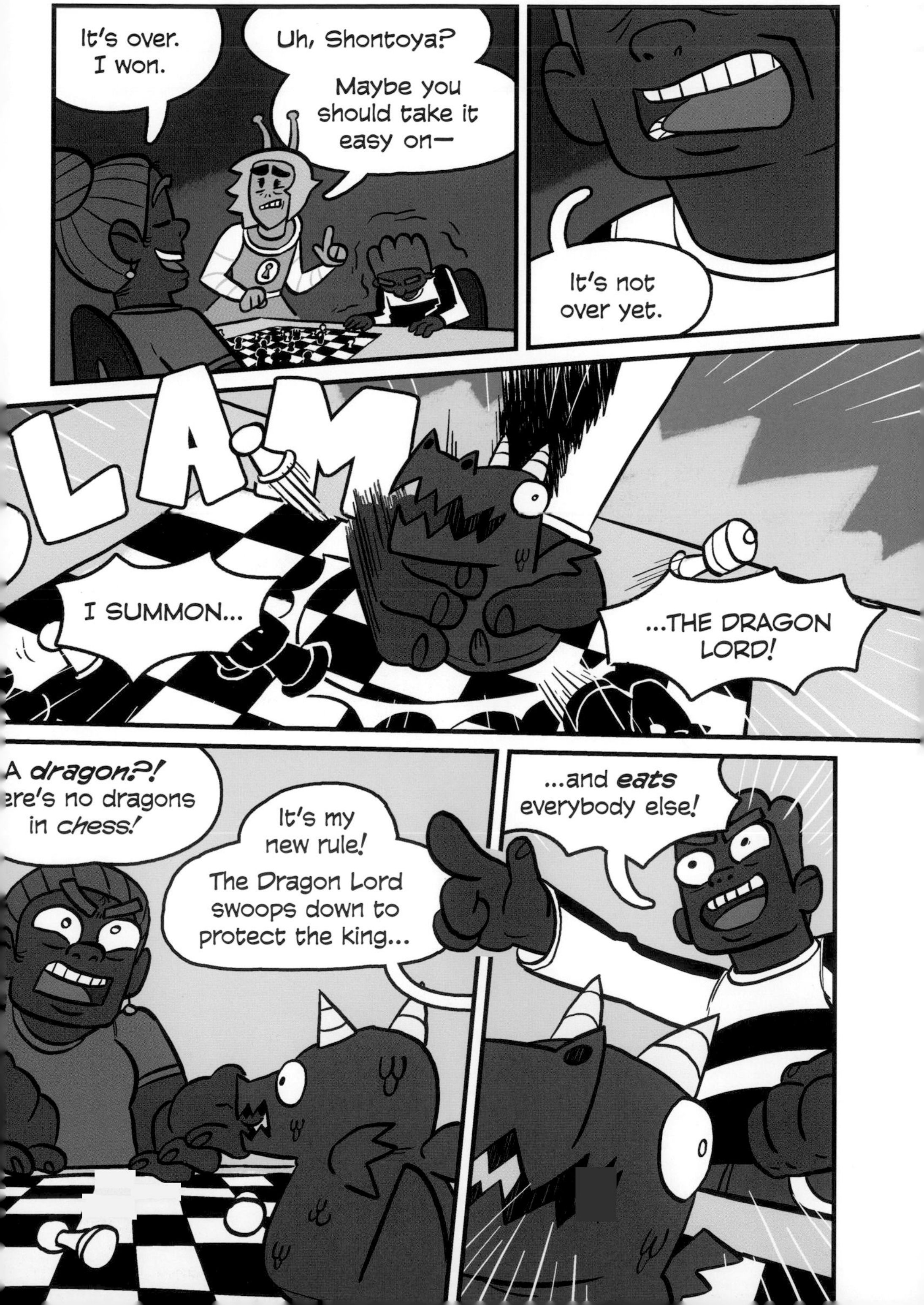
It's over. I won.
Uh, Shontoya?
Maybe you should take it easy on—
It's not over yet.
SLAM
I SUMMON...
...THE DRAGON LORD!
A *dragon?!* ere's no dragons in *chess!*
It's my new rule!
The Dragon Lord swoops down to protect the king...
...and *eats* everybody else!

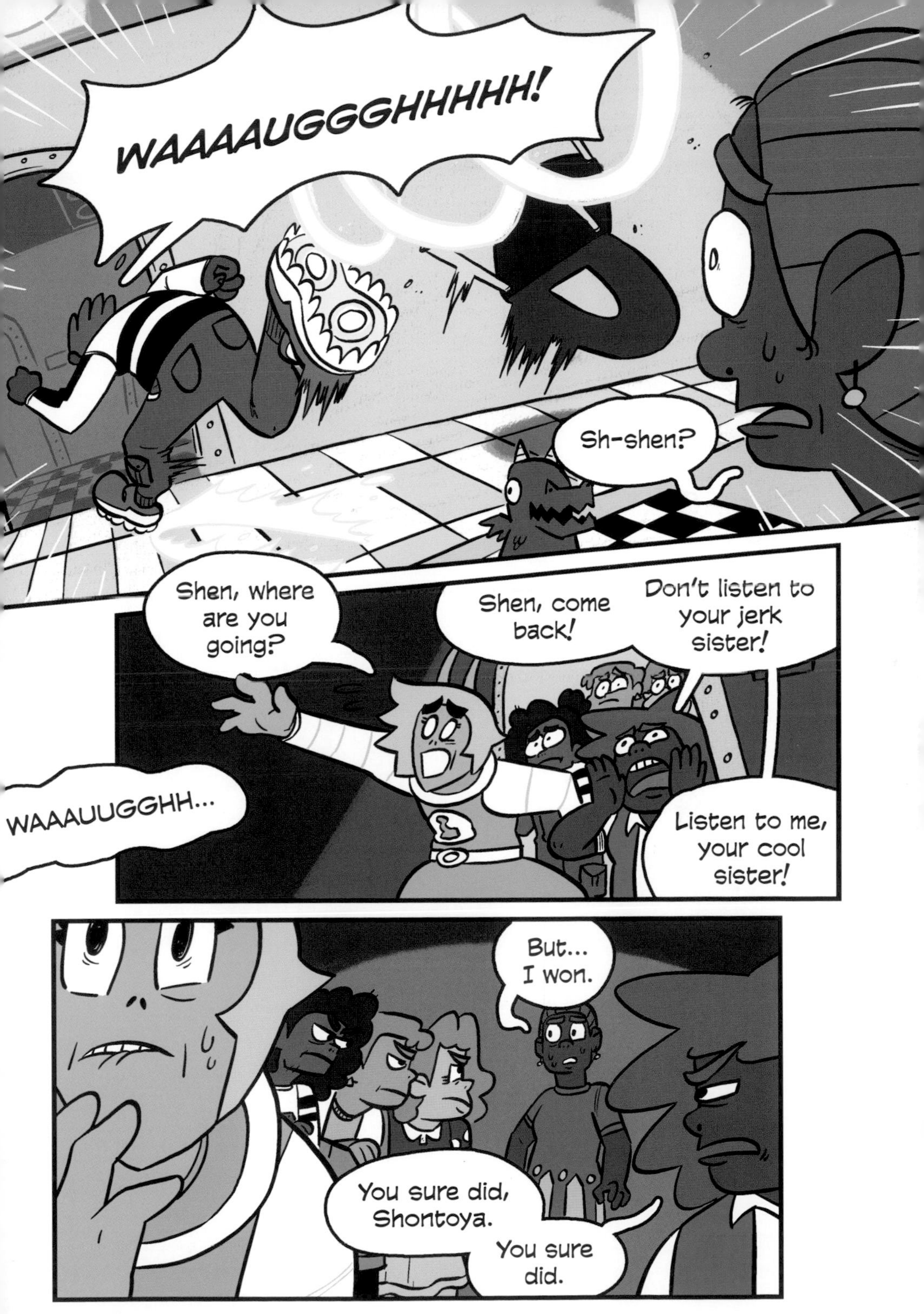
WAAAAUGGGHHHHH!
Sh-shen?
Shen, where are you going?
Shen, come back!
Don't listen to your jerk sister!
WAAAUUGGHH...
Listen to me, your cool sister!
But... I won.
You sure did, Shontoya.
You sure did.

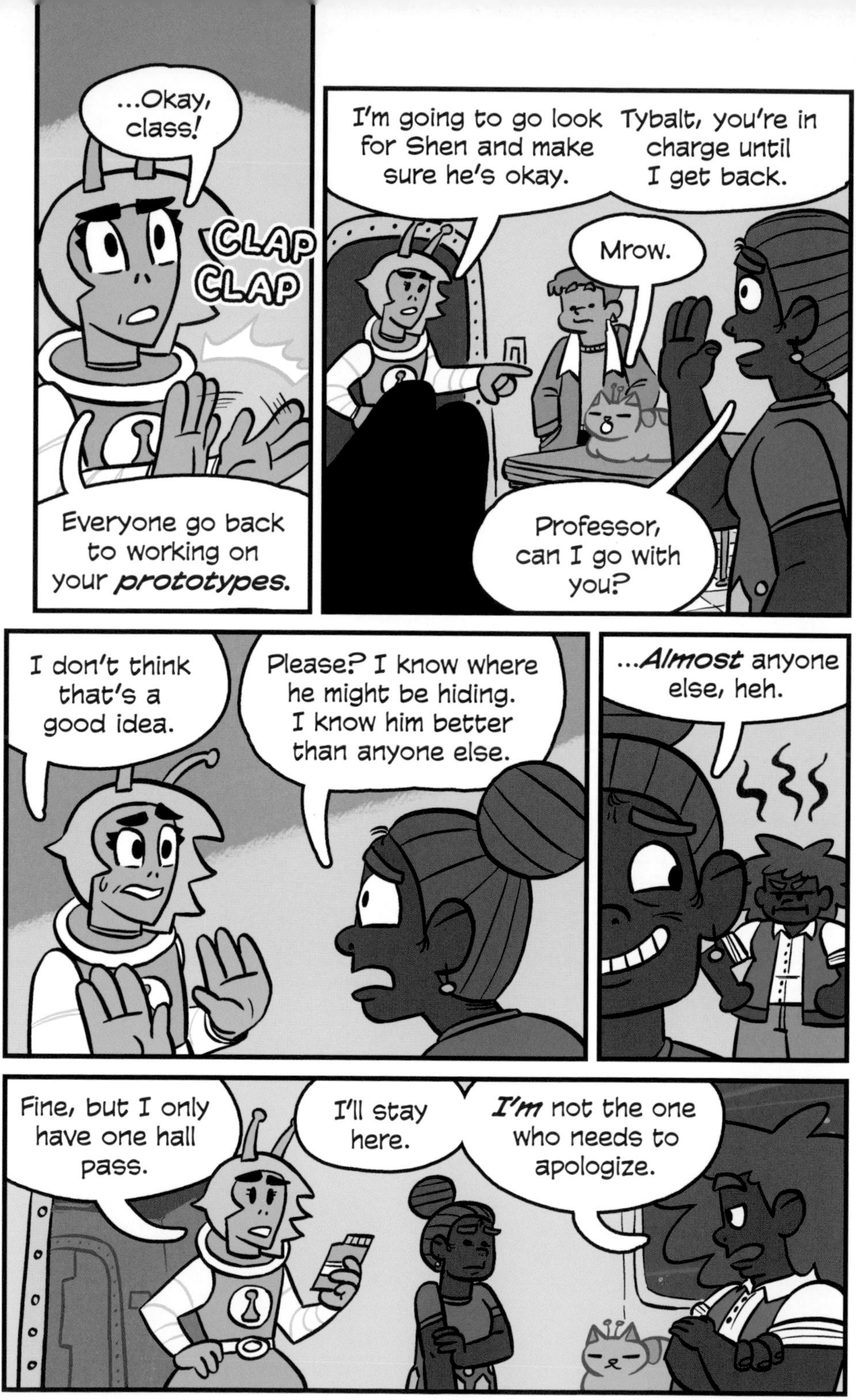
...Okay, class!
CLAP CLAP
Everyone go back to working on your *prototypes.*
I'm going to go look for Shen and make sure he's okay.
Tybalt, you're in charge until I get back.
Mrow.
Professor, can I go with you?
I don't think that's a good idea.
Please? I know where he might be hiding. I know him better than anyone else.
...*Almost* anyone else, heh.
Fine, but I only have one hall pass.
I'll stay here.
I'm not the one who needs to apologize.

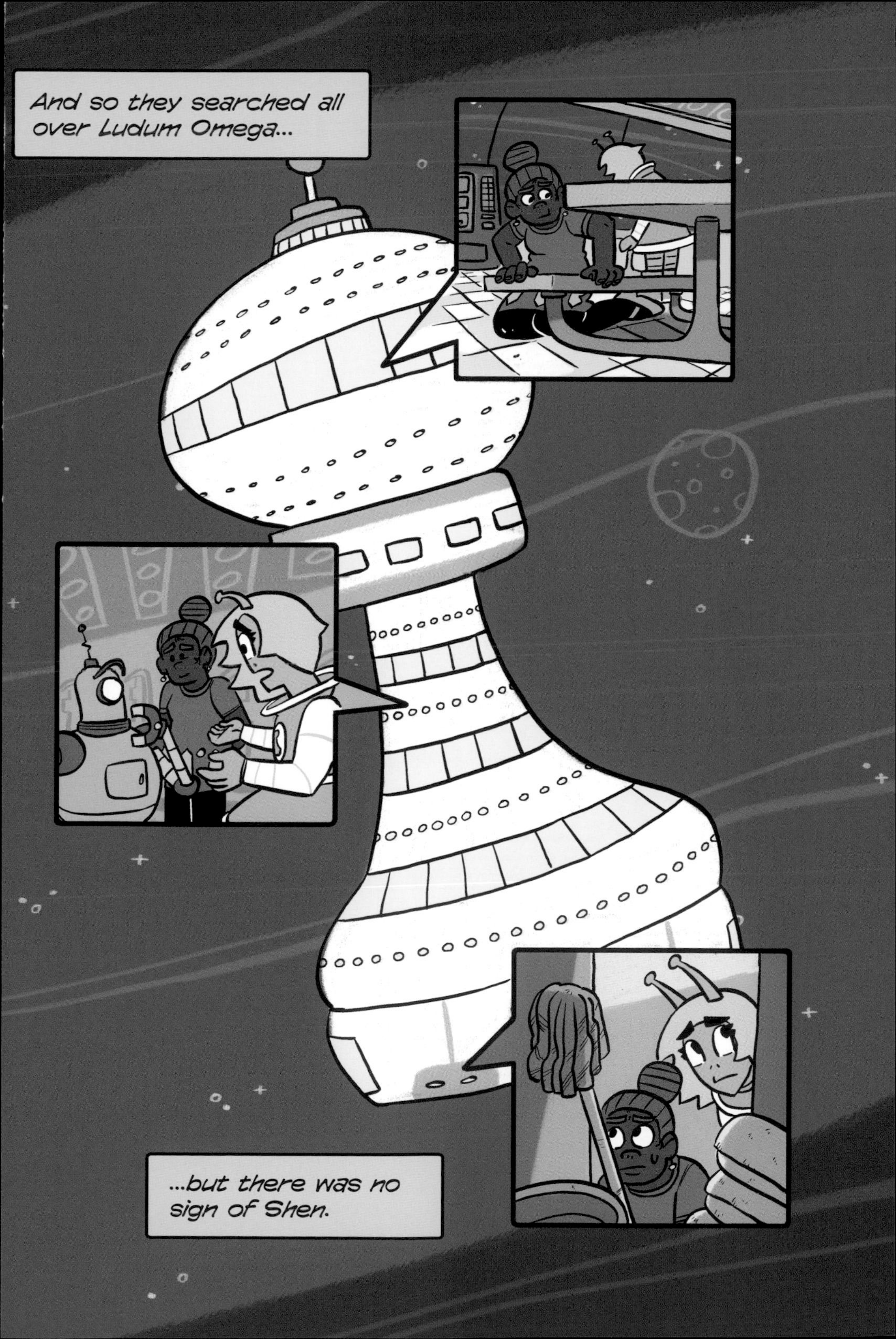
And so they searched all over Ludum Omega...
...but there was no sign of Shen.

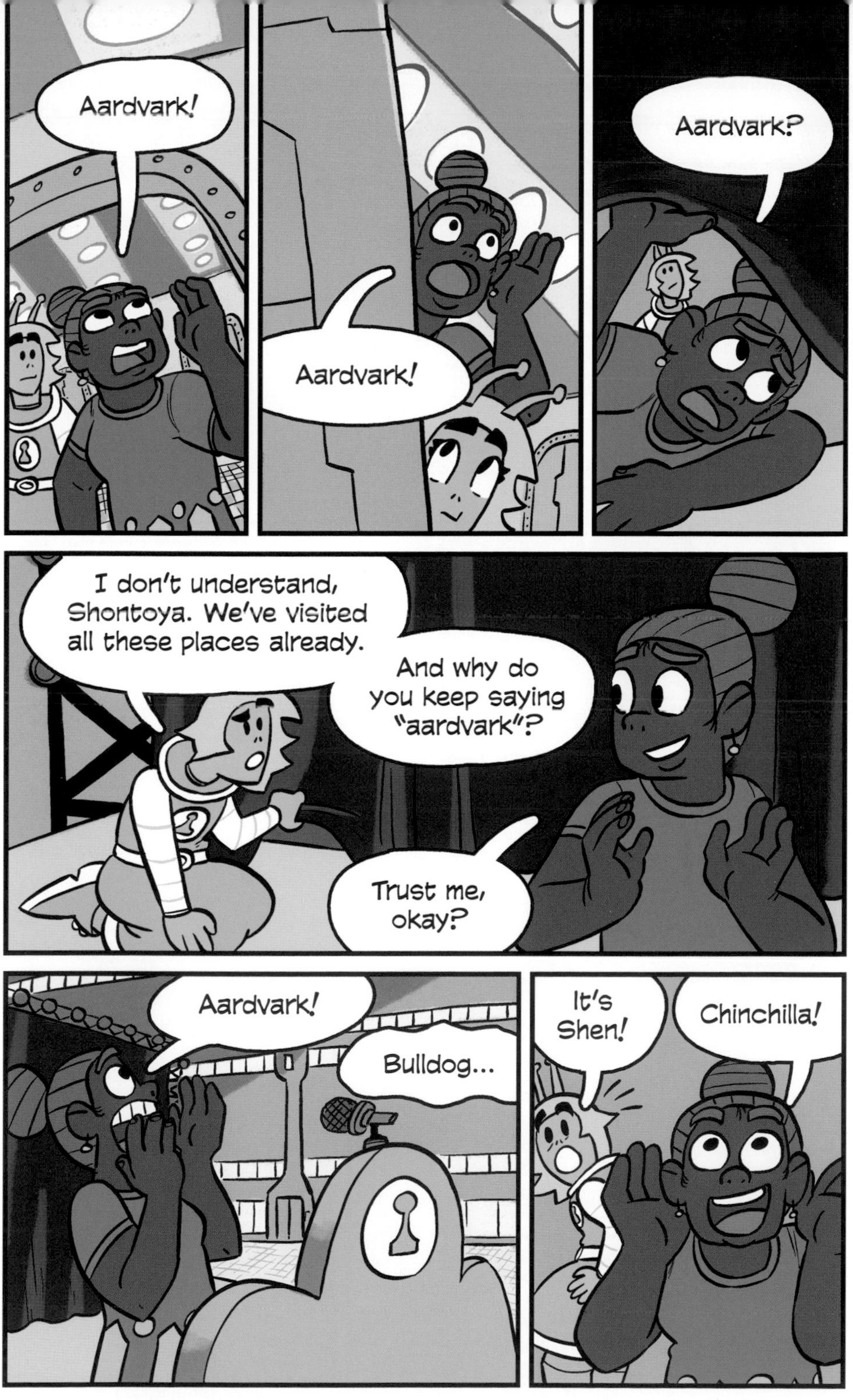
Aardvark!
Aardvark!
Aardvark?
I don't understand, Shontoya. We've visited all these places already.
And why do you keep saying "aardvark"?
Trust me, okay?
Aardvark!
Bulldog...
Chinchilla!
It's Shen!

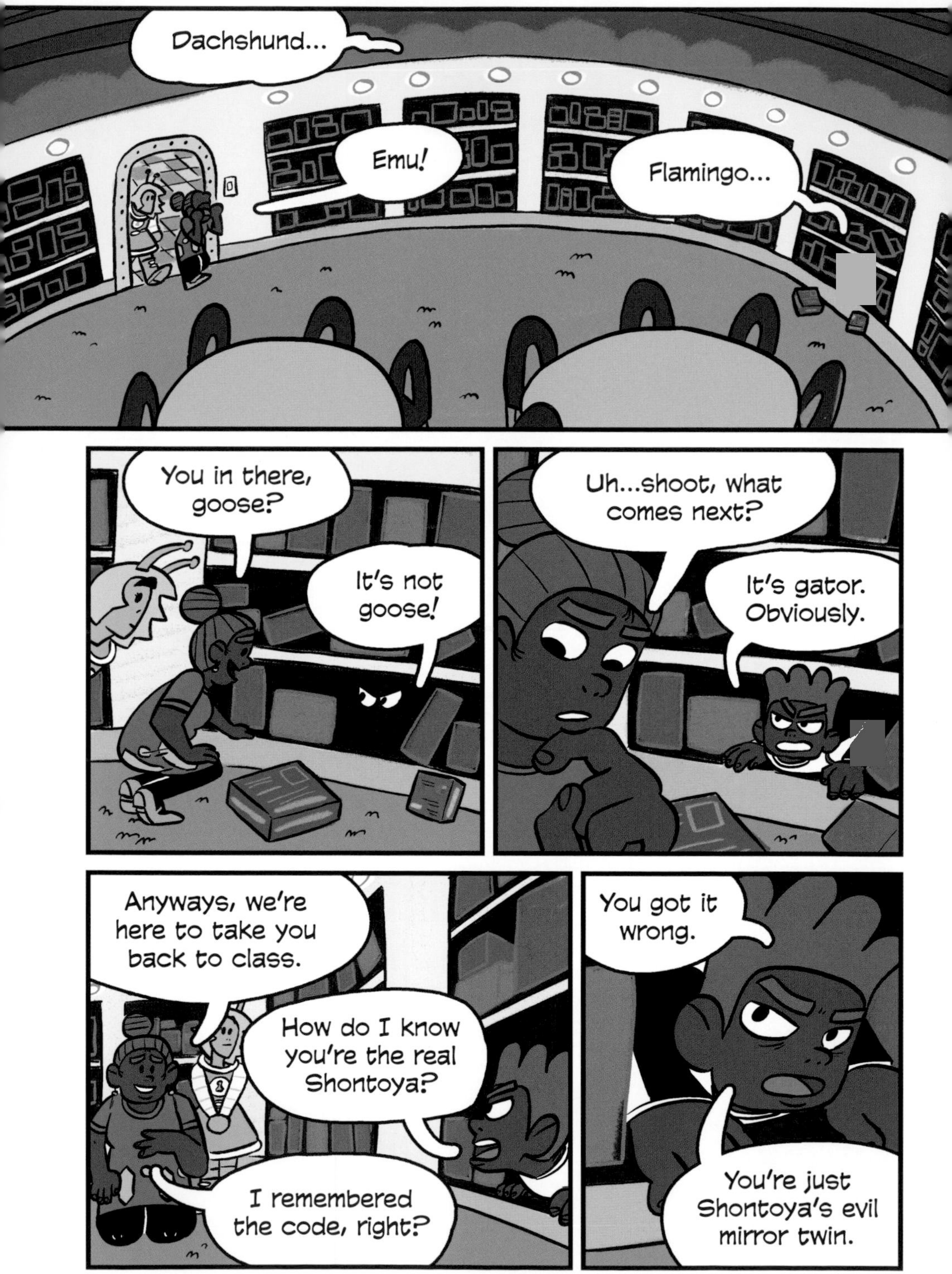
Dachshund...
Emu!
Flamingo...
You in there, goose?
It's not goose!
Uh...shoot, what comes next?
It's gator. Obviously.
Anyways, we're here to take you back to class.
How do I know you're the real Shontoya?
I remembered the code, right?
You got it wrong.
You're just Shontoya's evil mirror twin.

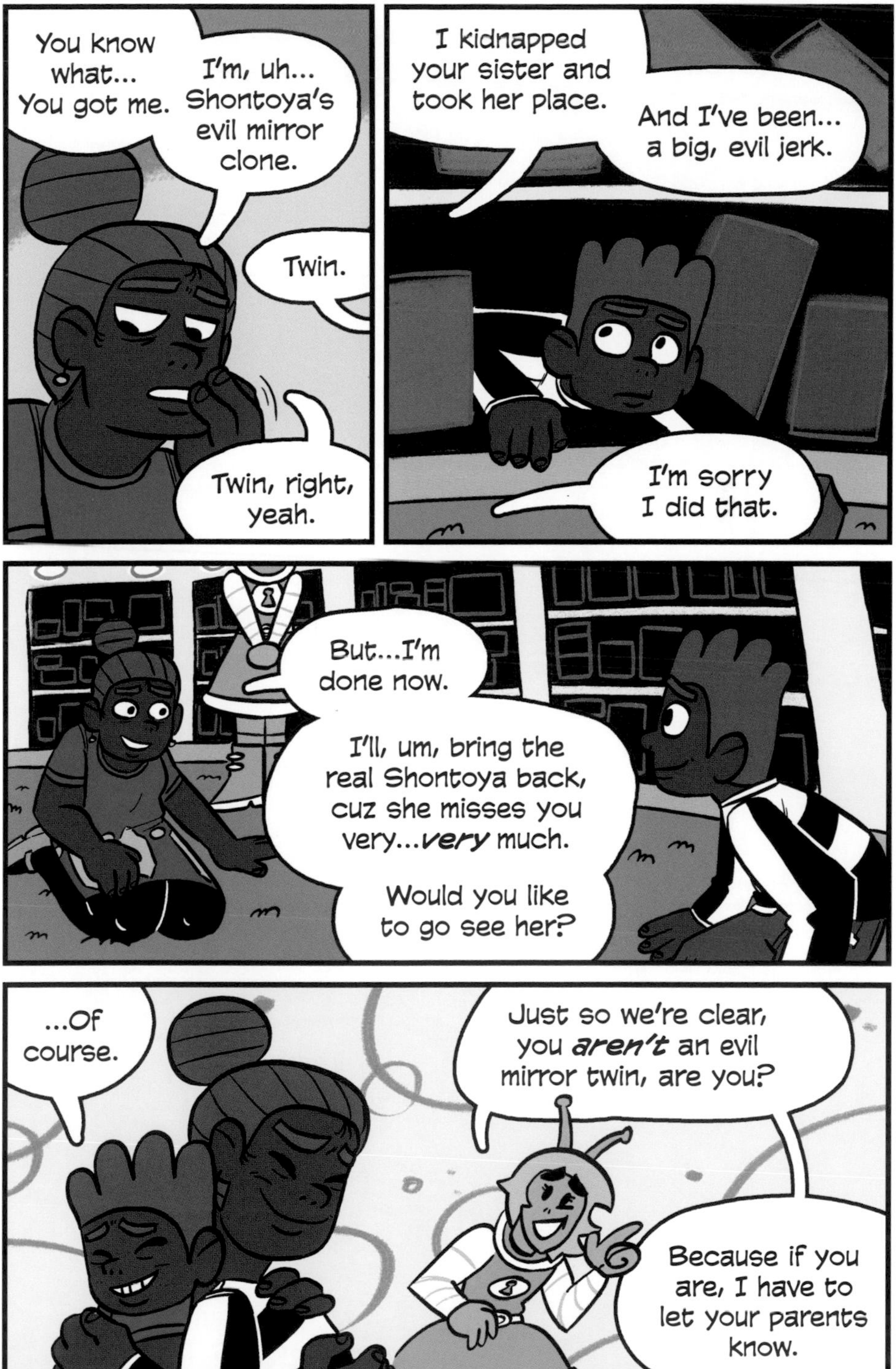
You know what... You got me.
I'm, uh... Shontoya's evil mirror clone.
Twin.
Twin, right, yeah.
I kidnapped your sister and took her place.
And I've been... a big, evil jerk.
I'm sorry I did that.
But...I'm done now.
I'll, um, bring the real Shontoya back, cuz she misses you very...*very* much.
Would you like to go see her?
...Of course.
Just so we're clear, you *aren't* an evil mirror twin, are you?
Because if you are, I have to let your parents know.

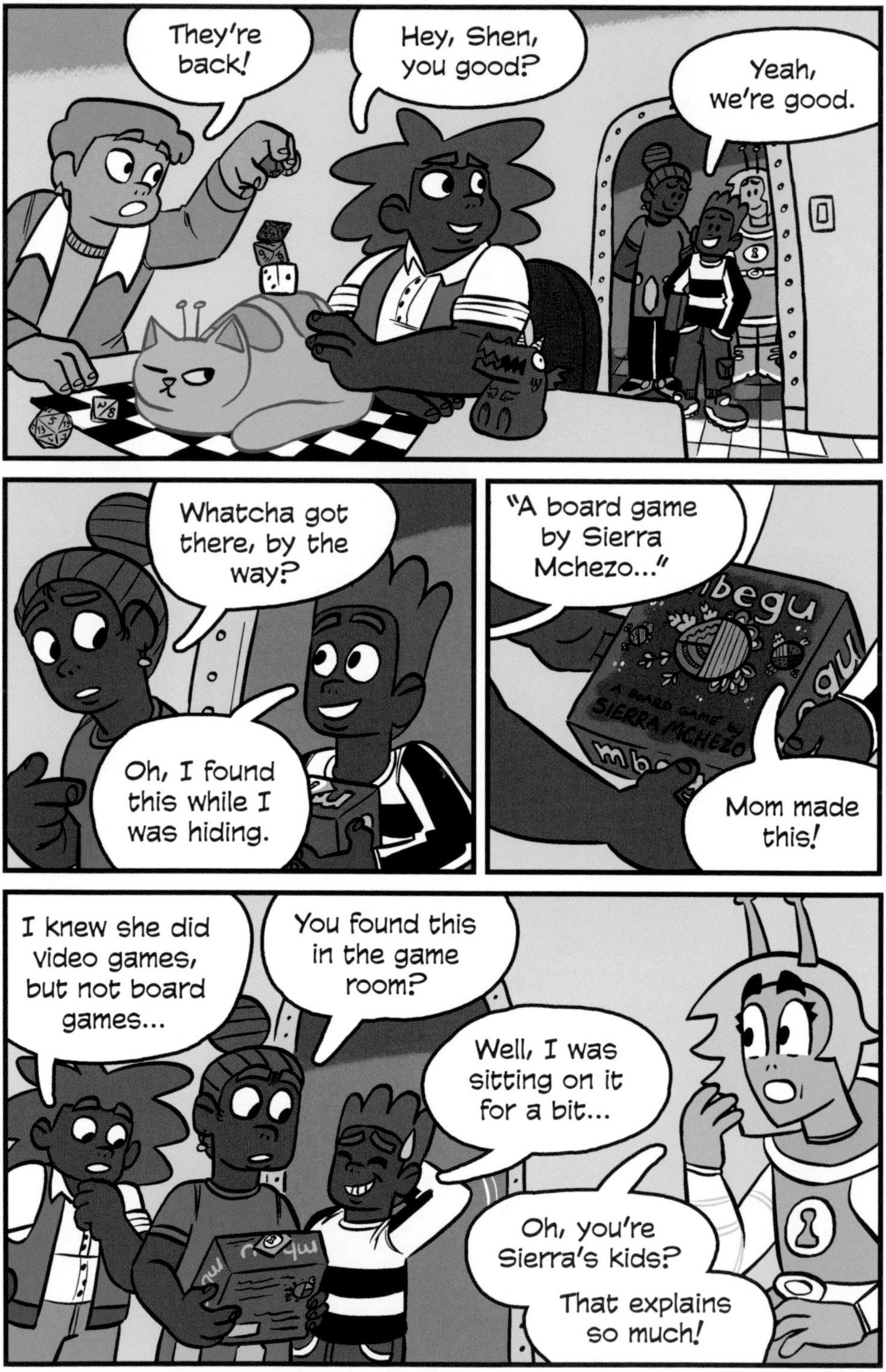
They're back!
Hey, Shen, you good?
Yeah, we're good.
Whatcha got there, by the way?
Oh, I found this while I was hiding.
"A board game by Sierra Mchezo..."
A BOARD GAME BY SIERRA MCHEZO
Mom made this!
I knew she did video games, but not board games...
You found this in the game room?
Well, I was sitting on it for a bit...
Oh, you're Sierra's kids?
That explains so much!

Let's Destroy *Chess!*

Players:	Materials:
2	Standard *chess* set, and whatever else you'd like to add!

This activity will be different from the others. Choose one or more options to flex your game design skills and turn chess *inside out!*

Option One: Change the Rules of *Chess!*

1. Each player chooses a single rule from standard *chess* to modify, or adds a new rule.

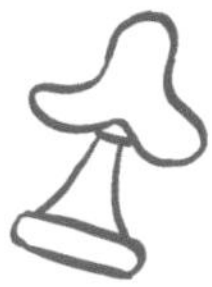

2. Write down your modification and read it out loud to your opponent. Answer any questions they have about your new rule, and make sure you understand theirs, as well.
3. Play a *chess* match with each player using their own modification. Then the players swap seats and try out their opponent's modification. How does this compare to normal *chess?*

Option Two: Alter the *Chess* Teams!

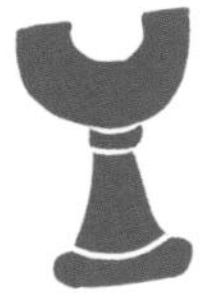

1. Each player builds a unique team of *chess* pieces, swapping pieces from another *chess* set. However, the players can only have one king piece each, and they cannot have more pieces than a normal *chess* team.
2. Play a *chess* match as both teams, swapping seats and noting how the changes affect your game.
3. Take note of how playing each team differed. Did one team feel harder to play against? Which pieces felt the most useful? How might you change the rules to work with these teams?

Option Three: Make a New *Chess* Piece!

1. Each player designs a totally new *chess* piece to replace a standard piece. What are its strengths? What are its weaknesses?

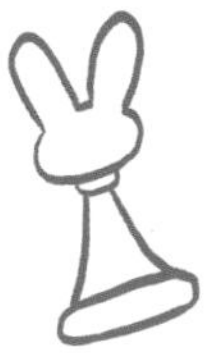

2. Each player makes an object to represent their new piece. They can make it out of any material as long as it fits on a single space of the chessboard.
3. Each player writes down their piece's rules and explains them to their opponent. Play a *chess* match trying out both new pieces. Then swap seats and play again. What is it like playing with or against the piece you created?

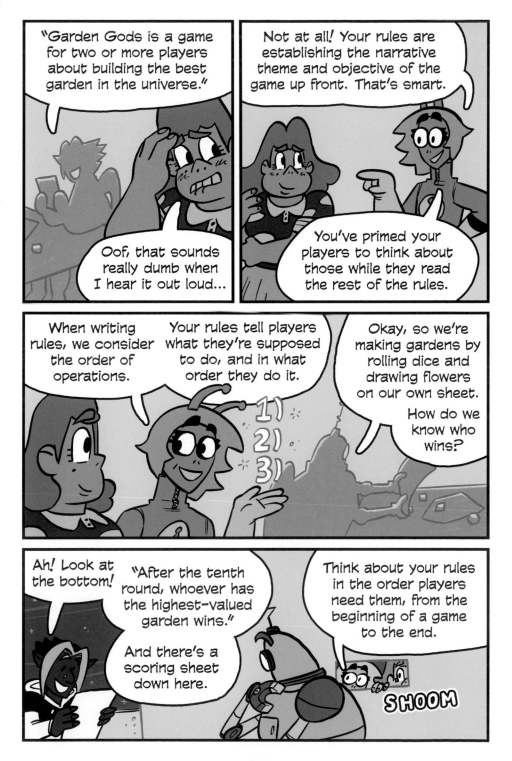

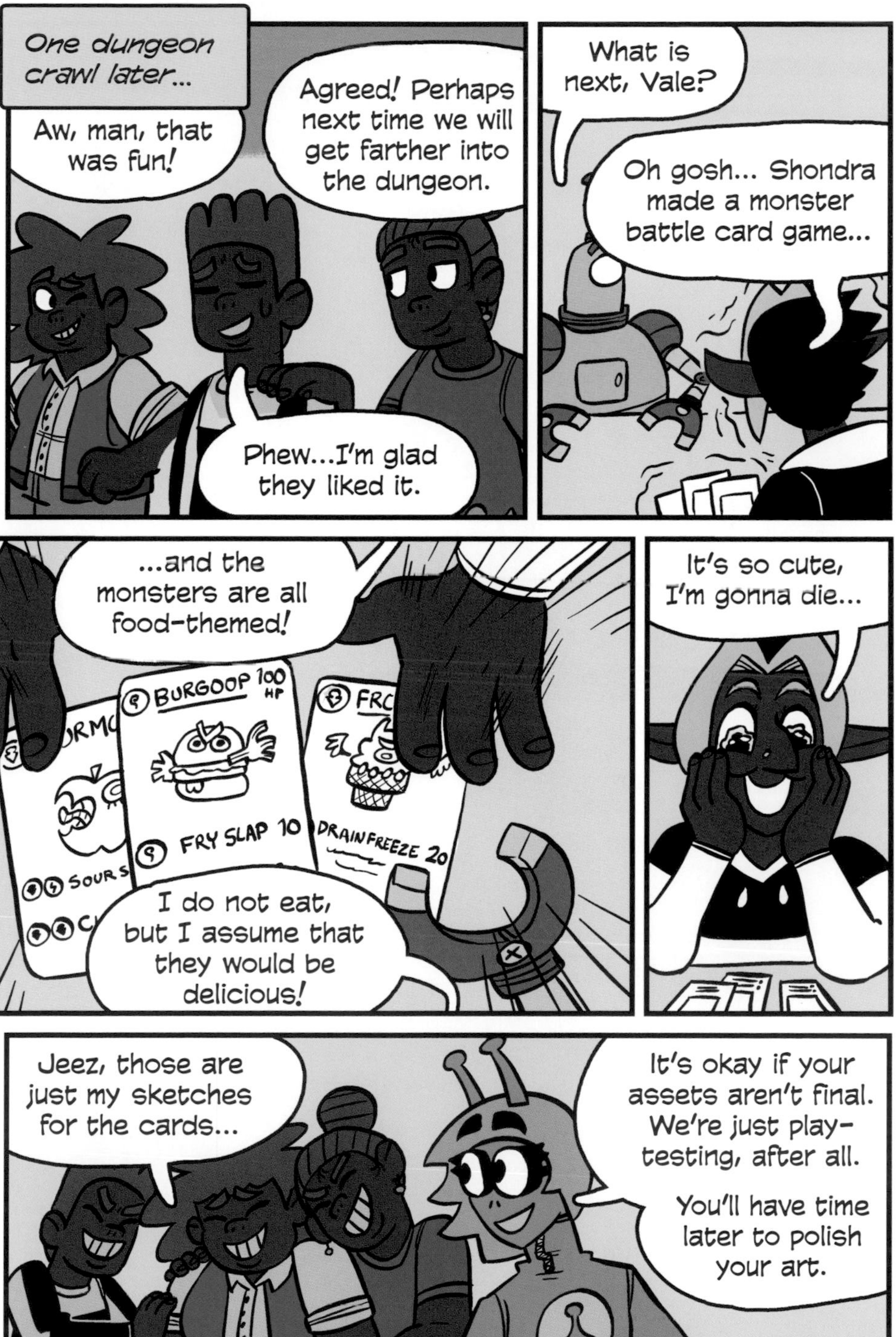
One dungeon crawl later...
Aw, man, that was fun!
Agreed! Perhaps next time we will get farther into the dungeon.
Phew...I'm glad they liked it.
What is next, Vale?
Oh gosh... Shondra made a monster battle card game...
...and the monsters are all food-themed!
BURGOOP 100 HP
FRY SLAP 10
DRAINFREEZE 20
I do not eat, but I assume that they would be delicious!
It's so cute, I'm gonna die...
Jeez, those are just my sketches for the cards...
It's okay if your assets aren't final. We're just play-testing, after all.
You'll have time later to polish your art.

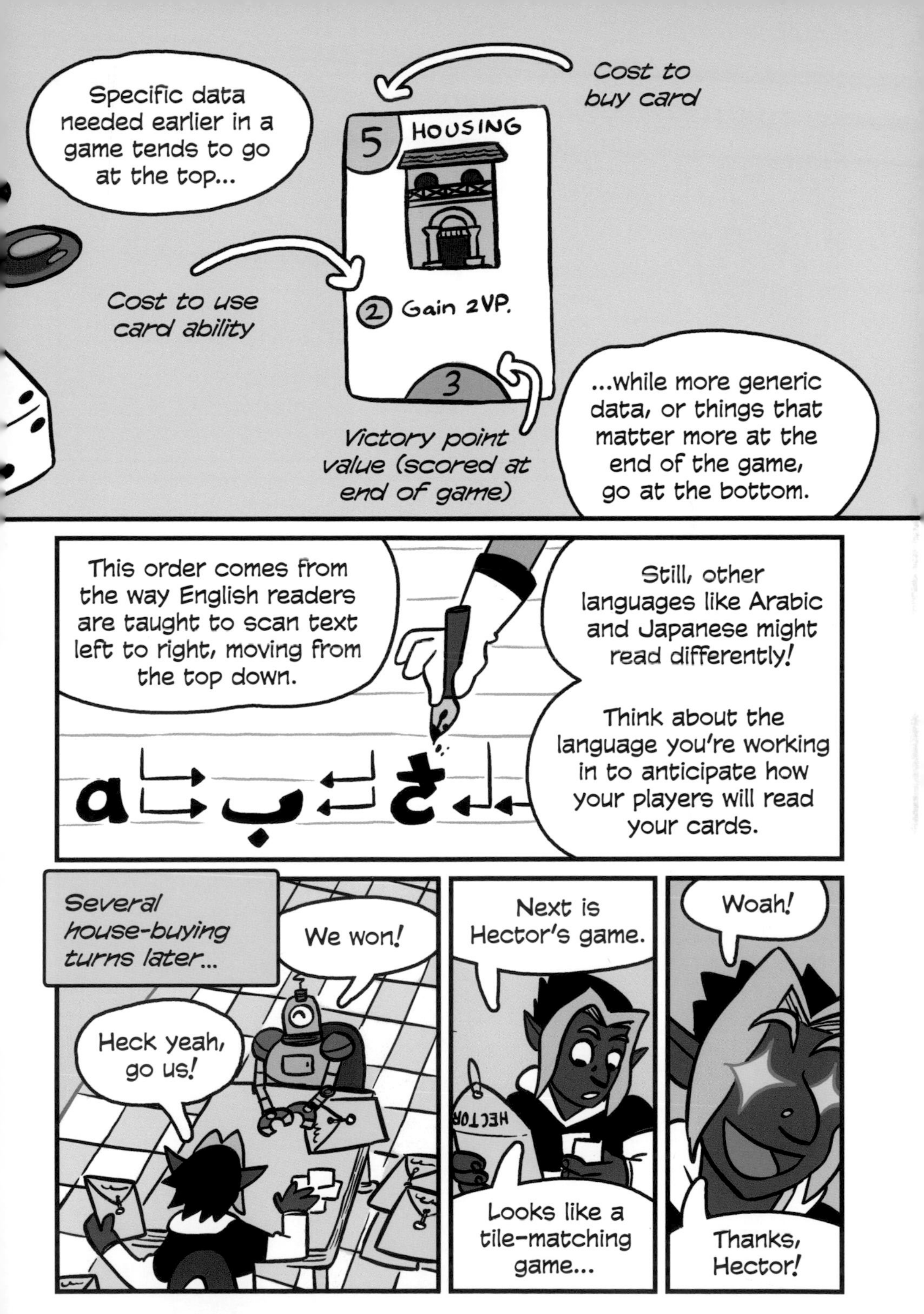
Specific data needed earlier in a game tends to go at the top...
Cost to buy card
5
HOUSING
2 Gain 2VP.
3
Cost to use card ability
Victory point value (scored at end of game)
...while more generic data, or things that matter more at the end of the game, go at the bottom.
This order comes from the way English readers are taught to scan text left to right, moving from the top down.
Still, other languages like Arabic and Japanese might read differently!
Think about the language you're working in to anticipate how your players will read your cards.
Several house-buying turns later...
We won!
Heck yeah, go us!
Next is Hector's game.
HECTOR
Looks like a tile-matching game...
Woah!
Thanks, Hector!

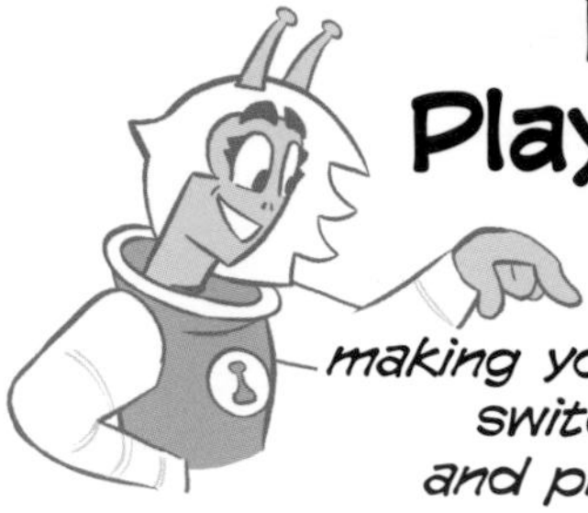

Prototype and Playtest Your Game!

Using your research in Day Four's brainstorming activity, you can begin making your new game a reality. Designers often switch back and forth between prototyping and playtesting, so feel free to do the same!

Part One: Prototype!

1. Write out your game rules. Try to sort your rules in the order that players will need them. Does your game have a theme? What can players do on their turn? How will players know when the game is over?

2. List your components. Your game can use dice and/or playing cards if you wish. If your game needs tokens, list how many your players will need. If you have original art, be as specific as possible with your list so you know what you need to create for your prototype.

3. Create any original assets needed for play. Remember that a prototype doesn't need to have final artwork or materials! You can make prototype components out of note cards, sheets of paper in plastic sleeves, minifigures from other games, etc.

Part Two: Playtest!

1. You can playtest a game by yourself! Try and follow your game's instructions and ask yourself questions while playing it:

   - "How is a single turn organized? What can I do on my turn? What limits are there on what I can do?"
   - "Why would I choose this option on my turn? Do I have too many options on my turn? Too few?"
   - "Does my choice affect what other players can do? How much do I ***want*** players to affect each other?"

2. Invite friends or family members to playtest your game! You can copy the feedback form at the end of this book for them to fill out. Ask them to play using your written instructions to ensure your rules are clear and concise.

3. Observe playtester reactions during the game and listen to their feedback. Discuss what changes you might try in future playtests. Happy designing!

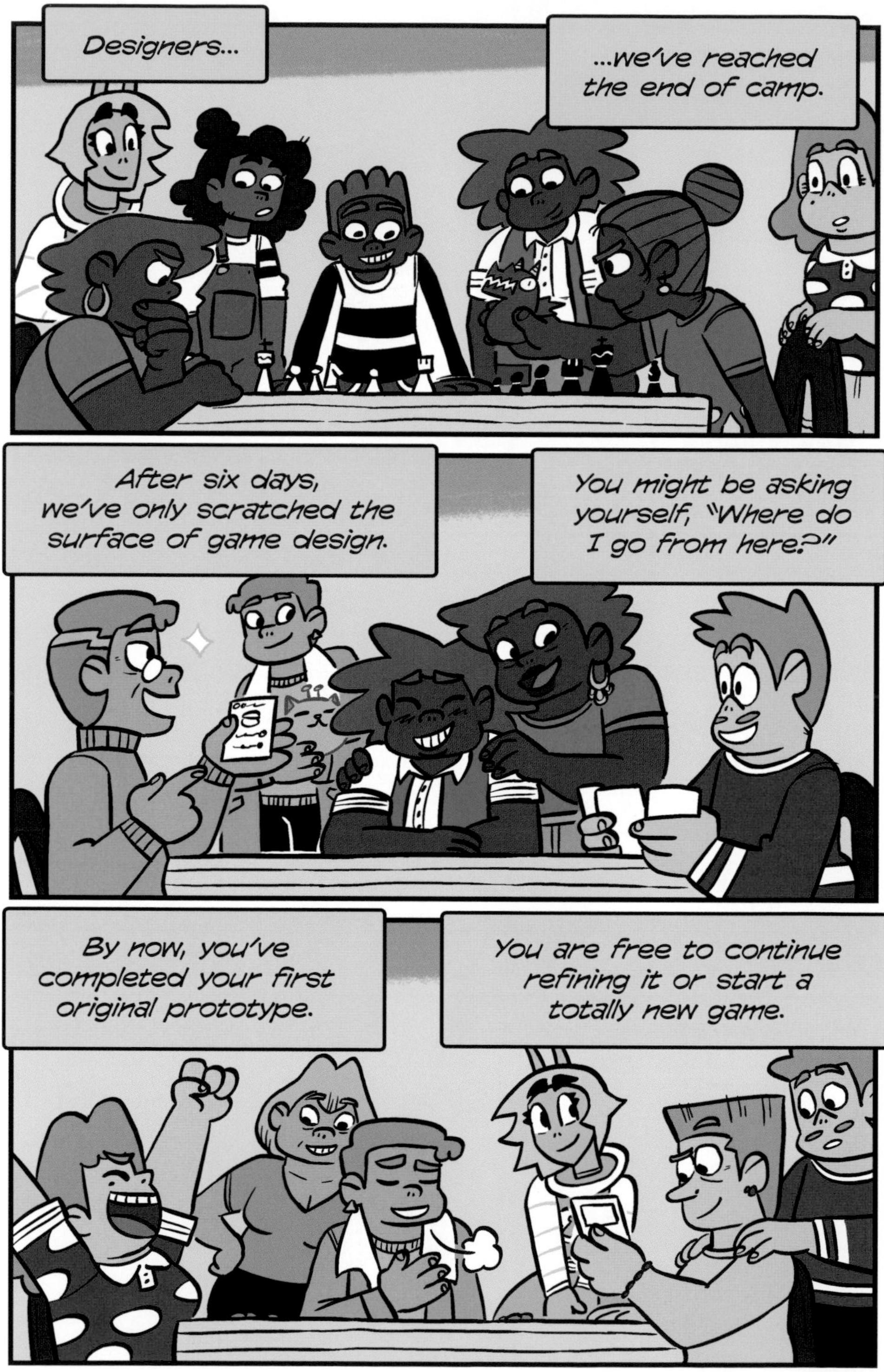
Designers...
...we've reached the end of camp.
After six days, we've only scratched the surface of game design.
You might be asking yourself, "Where do I go from here?"
By now, you've completed your first original prototype.
You are free to continue refining it or start a totally new game.

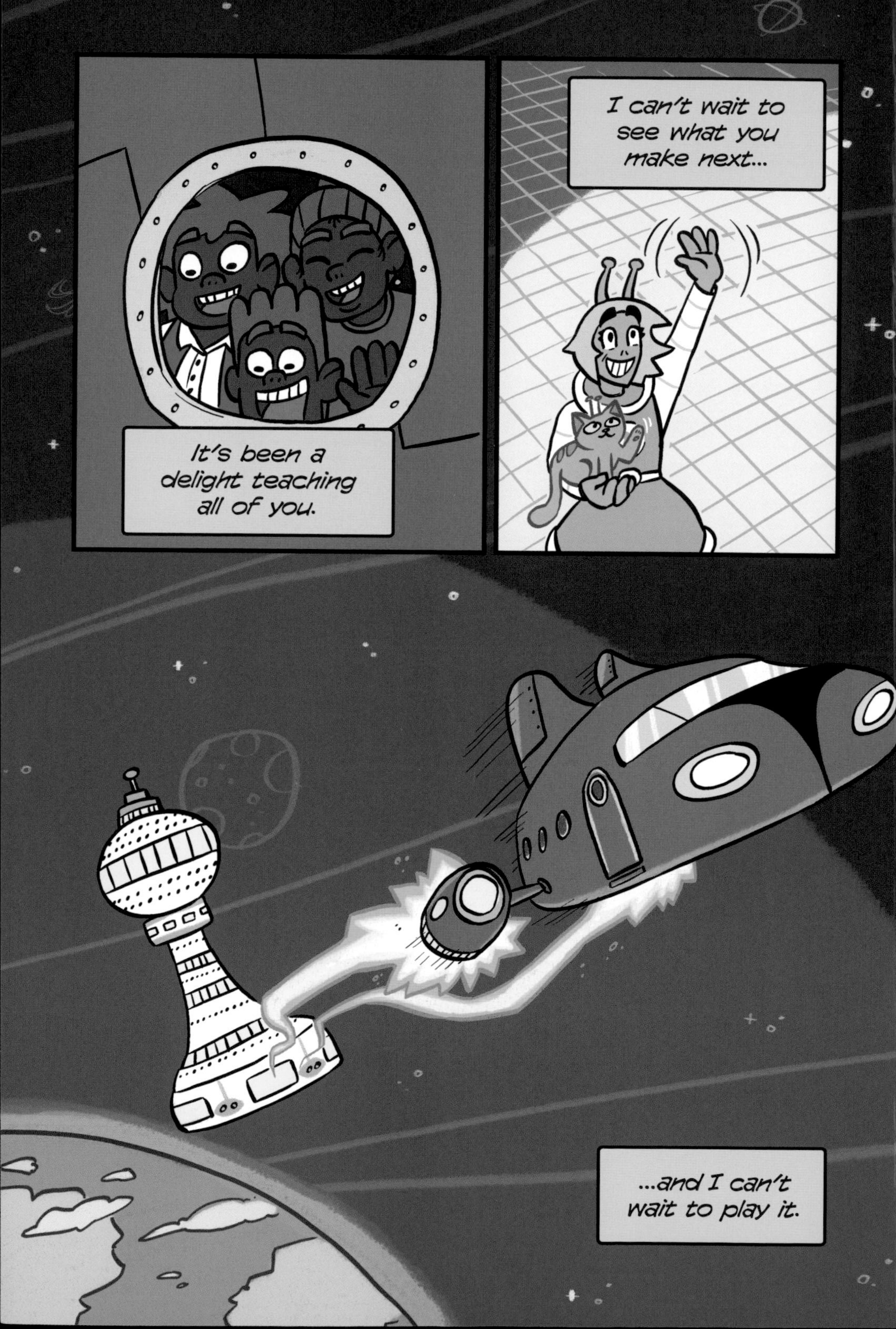
It's been a delight teaching all of you.
I can't wait to see what you make next...
...and I can't wait to play it.

GLOSSARY

Abstract: Distanced from reality. In games, a type of game with no concrete theming. Examples include *go* and *Hex*.

Card Memory: Type of component "memory" where one use affects the chances for the next. Examples include drawing a card from a deck or pulling a tile from a bag.

Component: A physical object necessary for a game such as dice, cards, paper, pencil, board, etc.

Connection: Game mechanic in which players complete paths or otherwise use adjacent pieces to achieve their goal. Examples include *Hex* and *Through the Desert*.

Dice Memory: Type of component "memory" where one use will *not* affect the chances for the next. Examples include rolling a die or spinning a spinner.

Mechanic: Broadly speaking, an action or choice you can make during a game in order to affect it. Games are often made up of multiple mechanics interacting with one another.

Module: A discrete set of rules that fit into a larger game.

Player Interaction: How much players can directly affect each other in a game. A game can be played with varying levels of interaction or even none. Examples of games with no player interaction include *blackjack* and *Ducks in a Row*.

Probability: A process by which one can measure the likelihood of certain outcomes.

Prototype: An early version of a game made for playtesting. Can also describe the process of creating an early version of a game.

Roll and Write: Game mechanic in which dice are rolled and players choose where to write the result on their personal sheet or board.

Roll and Move: Game mechanic in which a die, spinner, or other randomizer determines how many spaces a player can move on their turn. Games using this include *Monopoly, Candy Land,* and *Clue*.

Theming: Elements of a game that give it a narrative context. These can be illustrations, character designs, written lore, etc.

HEX RULES:

1) Each player traces two opposite sides of the board with their colored pencil. Flip a coin to decide who goes first.

2) Each player takes a turn filling in any empty space with their color.

3) The first player to connect their two sides wins!

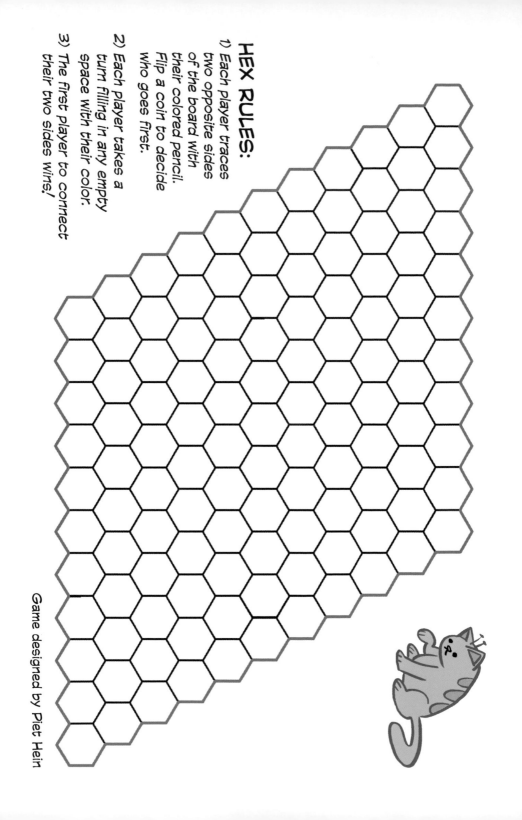

Game designed by Piet Hein

PLAYTEST FEEDBACK FORM

Name of game: Total game length:

First time playing? Yes / No   Did you win? Yes / No / Unsure

Write down any questions or comments you have during the game here:

	Least			Most
How clear were the game rules?	1	2	3	4	5
How strategic did the game feel?	1	2	3	4	5
How fair did the game feel?	1	2	3	4	5

What was a memorable decision you made during the game?

What did you do during other players' turns?

How did other players' actions affect your decision-making?

How did the theme affect your enjoyment of the game?

What new features might you be interested in?

What was the most enjoyable part of the game? What was the least enjoyable?

:01

First Second

Published by First Second
First Second is an imprint of Roaring Brook Press,
a division of Holtzbrinck Publishing Holdings Limited Partnership
120 Broadway, New York, NY 10271
firstsecondbooks.com
mackids.com

Library of Congress Control Number: 2022902112

Our books may be purchased in bulk for promotional, educational, or business use.
Please contact your local bookseller or the Macmillan Corporate and Premium Sales Department
at (800) 221-7945 ext. 5442 or by email at MacmillanSpecialMarkets@macmillan.com.

FIRST
EDITION

First edition, 2022
Edited by Robyn Chapman and Benjamin A. Wilgus
Cover design by Molly Johanson
Interior book design by Molly Johanson and Madeline Morales
Production editing by Dawn Ryan and Arik Hardin

Penciled and inked in Manga Studio, lettered and colored in Photoshop.

Printed in China by 1010 Printing International Limited, Kwun Tong, Hong Kong

ISBN 978-1-250-75052-5 (paperback)
3 5 7 9 10 8 6 4

ISBN 978-1-250-75051-8 (hardcover)
1 3 5 7 9 10 8 6 4 2

Don't miss your next favorite book from First Second!
For the latest updates go to firstsecondnewsletter.com and sign up for our enewsletter.